This book will introduce you to desktop publishing and shows you how you can create your own brochures, books and documents. It is primarily focussed on programs which operate under Microsoft Windows, although some are also available for the Macintosh.

There are many software programs which can help you. Unfortunately, there isn't a great deal of help available to advise you on which programs would be best suited to your needs. **This book is designed to fill that need.** It will not show you how to operate any specific piece of software but it will tell you the things which it can do and what its strengths are. In this sense, it is a concept book to show you what is available and how a program may be able to fill your specific needs.

First, you will get an introduction to word processing, fonts, file formats and the concept of WYSIWYG. It shows you what to expect from typical word processing programs. It covers the heavyweights such as *Corel WordPerfect*, *Microsoft Word* and some of the less popular programs.

You will be introduced to how colour is handled, especially by commercial printing houses. You will learn how to create portable documents which can be read on different computer operating systems and can also be used to prepare and send documents to commercial printers.

There are many introductory publishing programs which will enable you to create a wide variety of print documents and these are covered in a chapter called *"Soup to Nuts" Publishing Programs*. You will then be taken on a tour of the heavyweights in software publishing and layout programs which will help you to create books, newsletters, brochures and advertising material.

There is a chapter on some specialty programs which will be useful if you are engaged in publishing research papers or foreign language texts.

Voice dictation can save you countless hours of pounding at the computer keyboard and you will learn about some of the leading programs. In addition, you are shown how Optical Character Recognition (OCR) can help you scan and import written text on paper into your word processing files.

Finally, there is a chapter on the all-important topic of managing your documents. The book concludes by giving you a quick glimpse of the next exciting step in digital publishing; namely, how to publish your own eBooks.

Desktop Publishing for Beginners

How to Create Great Looking Brochures, Books and Documents

By

Learn2succeed.com
Incorporated

Published by:
PRODUCTIVE PUBLICATIONS

ISBN: 978-1-55270-455-4

Written by:
Learn2succeed.com Incorporated

Published in Canada by:
Productive Publications, P.O. Box 7200
Station A, Toronto, ON. M5W 1X8
Phone: (416) 483-0634   Fax: (416) 322-7434
Canadian Web Site: *www.ProductivePublications.ca*
American Web Site: *www.ProductivePublications.com*

Front Cover Art:
Spider web adapted from copyright free clip art from *Corel Gallery 200,000*
Corel Corporation, 1600 Carling Ave.
Ottawa, Ont. K1Z 8R7

Copyright © 2012 by Learn2succeed.com Incorporated

Library and Archives Canada Cataloguing in Publication

Desktop publishing for beginners : how to create great looking brochures, books and documents / Learn2succeed.com Incorporated.

Issued also in electronic format.
ISBN 978-1-55270-455-4

1. Desktop publishing. I. Learn2succeed.com Inc

Z244.64.D47 2012   686.2'2544416   C2012-903476-2

686.
2254
4416
DES

Disclaimer

No representation is made with respect to the accuracy or completeness of the contents of this book and both the author and the publisher specifically disclaim any implied warranties of merchantability or fitness for any particular purpose and in no event shall either be liable for any loss of profit or any other commercial damage, including but not limiting to special, incidental, consequential or other damages.

Throughout this book, reference is made to many different software programs; the names of which bear registered trademarks belonging to various software publishers. For the sake of making the text easier to read (as is customary in product review articles), most of these are shown without including the Trade Mark or Registered symbols. The absence of these symbols is not intended to imply any disrespect or disregard relating to the legal ownership of such trademarked or registered names.

CONTENTS

INTRODUCTION
What is Desktop Publishing?

Chapter 1
Fonts and WYSIWYG

Chapter 2
The Basics of Word Processing

Chapter 3
File Formats

Chapter 4
WordPerfect

Chapter 5
Microsoft Word

Chapter 6
Some of the Smaller Players in Word Processing

Chapter 7
The Role of Colour in Offset
and Digital Printing

Chapter 8
Creating Portable Documents

Chapter 9
The "Soup to Nuts" Publishing Programs

Chapter 10
The Heavyweights of Desktop Publishing

Chapter 11
The Leaders in Design and Layout

Chapter 12
Some Speciality Programs that Can Help

Chapter 13
Some Help with Creating or Importing Text

Chapter 14
Document Management

Chapter 15
When Gutenberg Turned in His Grave

INTRODUCTION

What is Desktop Publishing?

A Blurry Line

It's difficult to draw the line between the place where word processing ends and desktop publishing begins. The greatly enhanced features of the most recent versions of word processing programs enable them to do many of the things that were previously associated with desktop publishing software. I will therefore leave it to purists to draw their own lines in the sand about where one ends and the other begins, but for the purposes of this book I will examine the desktop publishing as being that software which enables you to create multi-page documents that are to be printed as a book or booklet.

A somewhat blurry line also extends the meaning of desktop publishing to include catalogues and brochures, business cards, greeting cards and even label designs. So, in an attempt to pacify those who feel that these creations should be included, I'll briefly cover some software applications which may be of interest.

The subject of pagination is one of the most obvious that relates to books or booklets and the major word processing programs are capable of generating page numbers at the bottom or top of each page as it is generated. Most can create tables of contents. This is done by associating a special code with each heading (or sub-heading).

Many books or booklets also contain headers or footers on each page. Thus, this book features the book title on every even-numbered page and the chapter heading on every odd-numbered page, with the exception of the first page in each chapter, on which the header is omitted. I should caution you, this will not be the case if your are reading this as an eBook in ePub format, but it will apply to the print-on-paper version as well as the eBook PDF version.

Where desktop publishing software comes into its own is in the areas of manipulating long documents containing large amounts of text or documents with lots of graphics. Most of the high-end desktop publishing software programs permit index tables to be created and will allow cross referencing of text within books or documents.

Chapter 1

Fonts and WYSIWYG

A Brief Word About Fonts

I would like to make a distinction between the basic types of fonts, since every desktop publishing document which you create will involve them.

Dating back to the Gutenberg printing press of 1436, lead type was set out on a tray, smeared with ink and paper then pressed against it to create a printed page. Over time this process became highly automated.

The alphabet of lead type had to be created in different sizes and styles so that a human typesetter could lay out the letters for each word individually; one page at a time. The typesetter had to have at his disposal alphabets of letters in different sizes (measured in points), in bold and in italics. Each of these collections of individual letters were known as a "font". In addition, many different styles of fonts were developed over the years.

As you know, the whole printing industry has changed; typesetters have gone extinct and lead type is no longer used. We are now in the digital age, however, the concept of a font is still with us and from a publishing viewpoint it is important to distinguish between different kinds of fonts.

PostScript Fonts

PostScript Fonts were first introduced by Adobe in 1984. They were precise font sets similar to the lead type fonts. They involved a scalable font technology which helps to make the appearance on your monitor similar to that on the printed page. This is true for Type 1 Postscript fonts; however, in the case of Type 3, they usually consist of elaborate designs which frequently involve bitmaps (i.e., series of dots) so they are not scalable (i.e., you can't readily enlarge or reduce them). Unfortunately, their use was licenced and many considered the licensing fees to be excessive. If you purchase a postscript computer printer, you will likely find that some of the most popular fonts are included.

TrueType Fonts

TrueType Fonts were first introduced by Apple in 1991 and later adopted by Microsoft. They allowed the sizes of letters to be scaled. They became very popular from the get-go since they were not subject to licence fees. You will now find over 6,000 different styles.

WYSIWYG

WYSIWYG (pronounced "Wiz-E-Wig") is an acronym for "What You See is What You Get". In essence, it lets you see on your computer monitor, the text that you have entered on your keyboard in word processing (or other programs) in a similar way to how it will be printed on your computer printer. You will note that I used the words "in a similar way" since your computer printer may not be able to reproduce a specific font unless it is programmed to do so. For example, your may type text

4

using a Helvetica font, but your computer printer may not be able to handle it and may substitute Arial, which is a TrueType font, in its place. Unless your are a purist, you probably won't notice much difference but this may not always be the case, especially with exotic fonts where the difference can be quite stark.

Chapter 2

The Basics of Word Processing

What is "Word Processing"?

Word processing is the most popular application for personal computers and you will probably be familiar with the features of specific software. In essence, it is the creation, input, editing and production of texts through the use of a computer system. It is also an integral part of desktop publishing.

Some of the Basic Features to Expect in Most Word Processing Programs

I'll describe some of the basic features that you would expect to be present in any word processing program.

Font Selection: where you can select the font you wish to use in a document. Also whether you want it in bold, italic or underlined and you can specify the colour of the letters.

Headings: provide you with the ability to create headings with different levels of priority. Thus, you could create heading No. 1 in Helvetica bold 14 point, and have it positioned and centred horizontally. Heading No. 2 could be a sub-heading created in Helvetica 12 point, bold italic. The body text could be in Times New Roman 12 point regular.

Heading in Arial Bold 14 Point

Sub-heading Created in Arial 12 Point, Bold Italic

The body text could be in Times New Roman 11 point regular.

Once these headings and body text styles have been established, they can be maintained throughout the document.

Headers and Footers: you can create a header and a footer which will appear on each page or alternatively you can specify only for odd or even pages, so that you can have different ones for odd-numbered pages and even pages. You can also suppress either of them on a particular page.

Justification: allows you to have the text on your page fully justified (as on this page), left or right justified or centred (such as in the bold heading illustrated in the previous text.

Page Numbering: is usually offered in a number of styles and you can reset the number if required.

Margins: allow you to set the top, bottom and side margins for your document and to change them on specific pages.

Tabs and Indentations: can be set on a ruler tab bar at the top of your page. These also allow you to indent your text.

Bullet Points: come in various styles and permit you to split up a series of points:

- this is point number one
- this is point number two

Paragraph Numbering: in which sentences or paragraphs are numbered.

1. This is sentence number one
2. This is sentence number two

Inserting Text Boxes: best illustrated as follows:

> This is an example of a text box with a shadow outline. It could even have no shadow or no border, depending on your preference. Its size can be specified as well as its position on the page.

Inserting Photos or Graphics: again with or without a border. You can resize the graphic and position it where you want it on the page.

Clip Art: is included in some word processing programs but usually in limited quantities.

Common Symbols: are usually included e.g., ¢ © ®

Lines: allows you to draw horizontal lines, vertical lines, dashed lines and freehand lines. You can specify line thicknesses.

Shapes: permits you to add shapes or create your own. A "drawing layer" will allow you to draw graphics or objects on top of your existing text or clip art. In this way you can add colour, gradients, fills or patterns to produce the special effects within your documents. This feature can be illustrated as follows :

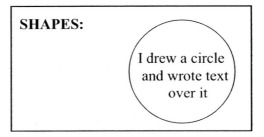

SHAPES:

I drew a circle and wrote text over it

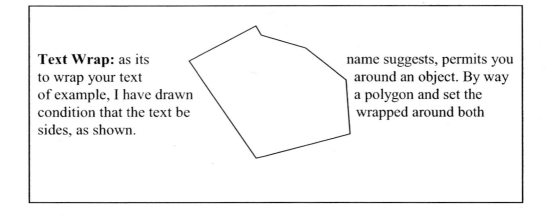

Text Wrap: as its name suggests, permits you to wrap your text around an object. By way of example, I have drawn a polygon and set the condition that the text be wrapped around both sides, as shown.

Tables: the ability to create tables allows you to size your rows dynamically within the table and to quickly join or split cells. You will see in the following table that the top cells of this three-column table have been joined; whereas the bottom left hand cell has been split into two. Again, you can specify thickness of the border right down to an individual cell.

This is an Example of a Simple Table		

Columns:

The text can also be placed in columns; the number and width of which can be pre-determined.

The space between columns can be adjusted according to the appearance which you want to achieve.

Widows and Orphans: occur when you get a single line at the bottom of a page or a top of a page. Most programs will allow you to keep the paragraph text together so as to avoid this.

Comments: where you can make a comment that will not interfere with your text layout and will not appear when you print a document.

Table of Contents: most higher end word processing programs will allow you to create a table of contents in a hierarchal manner for chapter headings, section heading, sub-headings and so on. You can also create bookmarks.

Hyerlinks: in which you can incorporate a Web address (url) and when clicked on, it will bring up that page on the Internet, assuming that Web browsing software has been installed.

Spell Check: permits you to check your entire document (or parts of it) for spelling errors once you have completed it. Most newer versions of word processing software will perform spell checks as you are typing and alert you to a word that has been incorrectly spelt.

Grammar Check: takes spell checking to a higher level but I must confess that I don't find this feature particularly useful.

Language: most higher end word processing programs allow you to specify the language you wish to work in. This is very important for spell check. For example in American English the word "color" is spelt without the "u" which appears in the Canadian English and UK English word for colour. Specify the language before you start or you'll go crazy!

Label Templates: most of the high end programs have label templates included so you can create your own labels for use on bulk mailings.

Search and Replace: enables you to search your entire document for a word or phrase and replace it with another. For example, if you have written a novel and the hero's name is Jim and you want to replace it with Chuck...it will do it for you...just with one click. On the other hand, if you just want to search your entire document for a word or phrase without changing it, the program will permit you to do this.

Macros: can be employed for repetitive tasks by instituting the keystrokes necessary to make a change. Thus, you might have created a document with three line spaces above the header and two lines below. For space reasons, you may want to condense the amount of space and reduce it to two blank lines above and one below. A macro will enable you to perform this effortlessly.

You could also use a macro with your name and address in it. So, every time you have a document that needs your name and address, you simply invoke the macro.

Be warned that only the higher end word processing programs offer this feature; however, it can be found in spreadsheets and other programs as well.

Kerning: allows you to manually adjust the space between two characters. The best way to illustrate this is by way of an example. If you look at the word "Yes" you will see a large gap between the "Y" and the "e". Kerning allows you to close the gap, thus: "Yes" in this instance closes the gap and is visually more pleasing.

Leading: refers to the spaces between lines and the term originates from the days when was being laid out for mechanical type setting. In those days, it referred to the strips of lead used to create the spacing between lines of text.

Drop Caps: are self-explanatory!

Mail Merge

Mail merge is usually associated with word processing rather than desktop publishing but I'll cover it here for the sake of completeness.

I'm sure you have received many pieces of mail where the envelope has been personalized, as has the salutation greeting on the letter inside. This is achieved through a mail merge where the data is maintained in one file and the template letter in another. The template letter has spaces left (and the necessary computer code in place) for the address information to be incorporated when a merge is commenced.

Mail merge can be a very powerful business tool but I am amazed that many business people fail to take advantage of it.

Chapter 3

File Formats

A Brief Word About File Formats

You are going to encounter the names of different file formats throughout this book, so I'll give you a quick description of some of the more common ones that will be discussed.

American Standard Code for Information Interchange (ASCII): is a code for representing English characters and numbers. Each is given a code which makes it possible to transmit data from one computer to another.

American National Standards Institute (ANSI): is the collective name for all code pages created in Microsoft's *Windows* operating systems.

Rich Text Format (RTF): is a format created by Microsoft for interchanging text in word processing between different operating systems such as DOS, *Windows*, OS/2 and Macintosh. As its name implies, it maintains the integrity of fonts in a document, such as bold, underline, italics, indentation, etc.

Portable Document Format (PDF): is a file format which was created by Adobe and permits documents to maintain their formatted appearance even when they are viewed on different computer platforms (PC, Mac, etc.) and when they are sent as e-mail attachments or are downloaded from a Web site. These files can only be read with an *Adobe Acrobat Reader* which is a free download from Adobe's Web site.

Extensible Markup Language (XML): is used to share structured data, especially on the Internet.

Open Document Text (ODT): is an XML-based file format used in word processing documents.

Encapsulated Postscript (EPS) Files: are image files which can be read by a PostScript Compatible printer, i.e., one which can handle PostScript fonts as well as images and graphics. This format is commonly used in the commercial printing industry.

Page Description Language (PDL): is used to describe the appearance of a page that is to be printed on a computer printer and is, in essence, a printer control language.

Hypertext Mark Up Language (HTML): is an authoring language for documents that you are creating for the Web. It consists of a large number of tags that can be used to format and lay out your Web pages. You should be cautioned that HTML can only handle a limited number of fonts and that the sizes are not fully scalable since you are limited to six different sizes, however, you can use bold and italic.

Extensible Hypertext Markup Language (XHTML): is very similar to both HTML and XML and has been described as a hybrid between the two of them. It enables layout and presentation to stay true to form over different platforms and is the code behind ePub, which is becoming one of the most popular formats used on a wide variety of portable devices for reading eBooks.

Standard Generalized Markup Language (SGML): is very similar in concept to HTML, insofar as it provides the rules for tagging, however, it does not specify any particular format.

HTML 5: is an advanced version of HTML which operates independently of *Java Script* (an object oriented computer scripting language which can be used to add dynamic content to Web sites) and *Adobe Flash* (a multimedia platform which is used to add video, animation and interactivity to Web sites) and eliminates the need for layout tags which are now replaced by Cascading Style Sheet 3.

Cascading Style Sheet 3 (CSS 3): is essentially the same as Cascading Style Sheets but are modularized to fit the needs of those who employ it without violating the standard.

OK-so let me try and cut through the geek speak and put all of this in simple language. It will mean that Web sites can be more easily created, designed and maintained and it will mean that video and audio can be incorporated more easily. It will also permit eBooks to incorporate multimedia. Furthermore, HTML5 has been designed in such a way that video and audio can be run on low power devices such as tablets and smartphones.

File Formats for Pictures and Graphics Used in Publishing

I will take a quick look at file formats for photos and images, since the names of these will be repeated many times in the following text.

Graphics Interchange Format (GIF): is a bit-mapped format that is very useful for transmitting images over the Web. It is better for scanned illustrations and animation rather than photos, since it achieves some compression by limiting them to 256 colours.

Joint Photographic Experts Group (JPEG) or (JPG): is a compression technique that discards information that the human eye cannot detect, however, unlike GIF, it can support up to 16 million colours and is suitable for transmitting photos over the Web.

JPEG 2000: is a more recent, updated and improved version of JPEG and it offers a higher compression ratio. In addition, it eliminates some of the "blurry" and "blodgy" features that characterized images in the original JPEG. It also offers better progressive downloads of images.

Portable Network Graphics (PNG): is another compression technique which can reduce file sizes by up to 25% more than GIF, however, it cannot support animation.

These formats are very useful since file sizes are smaller than is the case for other formats, and this in turn helps to speed up file downloads over the Internet.

Tagged Image File Format (TIFF): can be used for storing photographs, line art scanned images, etc. One advantage which this file format has over JPEG is that it can be edited and then saved without any deterioration due to compression.

Raw Files: refers to the image file formats in which pictures are captured in a number of cameras made by different manufacturers. It consists of the unedited, untouched pixel image (equivalent to a "digital negative") stored in your digital camera. If your camera can record in 12 bits of data, you can obtain 4,096 brightness levels (mathematically expressed as 2^{12}). If it records in 14 bit, then it offers 16,384 brightness levels (2^{14}).

Digital Negative (DNG) file format: is for archiving files generated in Raw format by cameras made by different manufacturers and also to accommodate the storage of pictures from cameras of the future.

Adobe offers a free converter which will convert Raw files from many popular models of digital cameras. Adobe is also committed to maintaining this format so that such files can be imported into any future software programs it develops, as well as the latest versions of *Photoshop* which are currently available.

Chapter 4

WordPerfect

A Leader in Word Processing

WordPerfect, published by Corel, has been a leading word processing program for many years. Unfortunately, it was slow to adapt to the *Windows* operating system and the first "Windows" version was so awful, I remember switching back to the DOS version. The good news is that those days are just a bad memory since, the program has since developed into a powerhouse of a word processing program.

The unfortunate aspect of the slowness to adopt, cost the program much of its market share and rival Microsoft *Word* swept the world with amazing speed.

Every time I attended a seminar when *WordPerfect* was being introduced, the seminar leader, in the introductory "rah rah" has always asked the audience what they like most about *WordPerfect*. In every case, the audience has responded by shouting "reveal codes, reveal codes!"

Reveal codes enable you to see the coding that creates the text which appears on your monitor. Reveal codes are displayed on the lower part of your screen and the area can be adjusted. Reveal codes are only partial coding since the actual code that creates each character is not displayed as this would produce a mass of gobbledygook which would be unintelligible for the average user. Instead, reveal codes show the code for such things as underlining, bold, italics, font sizes and styles, the hard return at the end of a paragraph or at the end of a page.

To be fair, Microsoft *Word '97* offered a rudimentary level of reveal codes, however, it was nowhere as elaborate as that of *WordPerfect* and this feature was eliminated in *Microsoft Word 2000* and more recent versions.

To many people, reveal codes are a distraction and they like to have them turned off. Indeed, I have been challenged on many occasions as to why I find reveal codes so important in word processing. I will attempt to answer by way of an illustration.

In addition to being an author, I also publish the books of many other authors and I receive their manuscripts on paper as well as saved on floppy disks or DVDs in various word processing programs. In most instances, I have to completely re-format their text so that I can lay it out in a form that is amenable to being printed as a book. The first thing I do once I have imported a file into *WordPerfect*, is to switch on my reveal codes and clean out all the unnecessary code so that I can format the document in a suitable style. I am totally amazed at the amount of unnecessary code that accumulates in some of the manuscripts that have been submitted to me in *Microsoft Word*. Without a powerful set of reveal codes, it is virtually impossible to clean up these manuscripts. Attempting to do so without reveal codes is akin to a blind person walking across a fast-moving highway and having no idea of where the next vehicle is and how to avoid it or what to do about it!

One specific case comes to mind. When I was working on a manuscript several years ago which had been submitted by the author in *Microsoft Word* format, there was a page where I just could not get *Microsoft Word* to obey any commands. In sheer frustration, I cut the page out and pasted it into *WordPerfect* where I found to my amazement, in looking at the reveal codes, a huge number of very small and unnecessary "left tab" entries. I did a search and replace "left tab code" with "nothing" and found there were over 400 left tab entries that had been eliminated–just on **one** page! I cleaned out several other code entries in a similar manner and then replaced the page back into the *Microsoft Word* document where it worked perfectly! In all, there were over 30 pages in that 230 page book which had to be cleaned up in this manner.

Most people do not use reveal codes and are quite happy living with their blindfolds on! At least, you should be made aware that reveal codes exist and they will often help when you can't "get that... blank... word... blank... processing... blank... software... to... blank... well work!" You may think that I am joking, but believe me, I have seen this scenario repeated many times!

WordPerfect excels at reveal codes. Enough said!

Another powerful feature of *WordPerfect* is the ability to control and track multiple copies of the same document. Thus, if you are updating a document, it is possible to save the updated version and compare it with the original version to see the changes which were made. Such changes are normally highlighted with red underlining to differentiate them from text that remains unchanged. This feature is particularly useful when a draft has been created and is passed on to numerous people for revision. Those revisions can be saved as separate files and compared to the original--a very powerful feature for collaborative work.

WordPerfect contains a template folder in which a number of useful templates have already being created and all you have to do is to personalize them for your particular situation. For example, there is a template for a business letter, fax, memo, newsletter and resumé. Also included is a calendar that can be customized as well as a sign template; enabling you to make your own signs for upcoming events.

One very powerful feature that is incorporated into *WordPerfect* is the timed backup. This will automatically backup the document on which you are working at regular intervals which you can pre-set yourself. The most common setting is at ten minute intervals which would mean that the maximum amount of information that would be lost due to a system failure or some human error would amount to 10 minutes of work.

The only downfall of this feature is when your file sizes become very large, such as when many graphics are incorporated into a document, it may take several minutes to save such a file, even on a fast computer. Since file saving is a very computer-intensive operation, you are essentially made to sit at the keyboard doing nothing while this operation is going on. If you work this out, and it takes 1 minute out of every 10 for backups, your productivity will be reduced by 10%. In addition, there is the distraction to your train of thought! So, in practice, I find that it is better to backup when I have completed a particular section. This gives me a short break in which to gather my thoughts before tackling the next section and gives me mastery over my computer as opposed to being its slave!

One very nice addition that was introduced with *Version 9* is the ability to preview your document in various font styles, without actually making any changes to your document. Thus, you can block out a section of your document which was formatted using the font *Helvetica Bold* and see what it looks like in *Bookman* or some other font. This will give you the visual appearance of your document without actually implementing the change. In this way you can look at many different font styles and see how they will apply to your project.

Up until *Version 9*, it was only possible to look at font styles in a small pull-down menu and you were not able to fully appreciate how your document would look since style was not applied to your entire document.

This new enhancement should be of particular interest to those who have to layout advertising and marketing brochures; where appearance is all-important. Obviously, it will also be of interest to you if you want to change the appearance of new documents that you are creating or ones that you have previously created.

Another feature enables you to save the fonts that you have used in your document and make sure that those specified font styles accompany the document, so that it will always have the same set of fonts; regardless of where the file is opened. This overcomes a problem when you move a document from one PC to another that does not have the same fonts installed and very often the appearance is changed. Now, when you send your document to another computer, you can be assured that it will maintain the same appearance.

An obvious exception to this would be if you use a "printer font" and the other computer printer does not offer the same font, this feature will not work. However, if *TrueType* fonts are used, the appearance can be maintained and this is a useful feature for documents sent as attachments with e-mail over the Web.

An "auto scroll" button is available on the toolbar which enables you to quickly scroll through your document; either vertically or horizontally, once it has been enabled. This is in addition to the traditional scroll bars that appear on the right hand side of the monitor when you're working in this program.

There is a "browse button" similar to that found when you're browsing Web pages. It enables you to go back to the previous page that you were working on. It is a very useful feature and something which I greatly appreciate; because previously, if you were working on a long document, you had to remember a previous page number if you wanted to return to it.

"Block-Make-It-Fit" is also a very useful feature which helps you fit the text which you have blocked onto a specific page or a specific number of pages. Previously, if you wanted to fit your text, you would need to block the text and change the line spacing or adjust the font size and if you didn't get it right the first time, you would have to keep fiddling around until you achieved the desired result. This feature will get it right the first time and can be a real time-saver.

An interesting feature that was introduced in *Version 9* was an enhanced charting ability. This will be particularly useful for those who have to come up with organizational charts. This places Corel *WordPerfect* in a more competitive position with Microsoft which purchased *Visio*, a charting product that works very closely in association with *Microsoft Word*.

Those readers who prefer to use keystrokes rather than a mouse to gain access to the features of this program, will be interested to know that keystroke shortcuts were enhanced commencing with *Version 9*. I must confess that this is a feature which is of little interest to me, since I am a devoted "mouse person"!

A large number of drawing shapes are available, such as arrows or star bursts; features which will be particularly useful in preparing brochures and other advertising documents.

It is possible to skew cells in a table. This is particularly useful for a column header that is quite large relative to the material below it. This means that the column header and the text within it can be skewed at an angle. If you have worked with tables you will recognize that this is a very useful feature.

If you are interested in distributing your documents in electronic format, *WordPerfect* enables you to publish them to HTML, XML and EDGAR (a format used for legal documents).

The versions, *WordPerfect X3* and *X4* let you import and export PDF files. This is a very powerful feature which was sorely lacking in earlier versions of the software. Version *X4* will automatically create bookmarks, e.g., if I save this book (created in *WordPerfect*) as a PDF, version *X4* will automatically create bookmarks in the form of tabs for each chapter–just as in a binder–so you can proceed directly to that chapter. In version *X4* you can also password protect your PDF documents and you can also import scanned PDFs, which essentially permits you to "unlock" the text so you can perform edits.

In version *X4*, you are offered a choice for the quality when saving your PDF file. This can range from lower quality with a small file size, suitable for use on a Web site to high quality (and large file size) which would be needed if you are going to send your work to a commercial printer.

These *X3* and *X4* versions let you copy and paste text from the Web and will automatically format it to match the text of the document you are working on. This is a very nifty feature!

It can also reformat your work to fit a predetermined number of pages. Also, if you have imported material from *Microsoft Word* , there may be commands which are not visible when you view it on your monitor. To overcome this shortfall, Corel has introduced a feature which lets you save your document and clears out everything which is not visible.

WordPerfect X4 will let you import documents in Open Document Text (.odt), Rich Text Format (.rft) and from *Microsoft Word 2007* and earlier versions (.doc .docx and .docm), and obviously Text files (.txt), ASCII and ANSII. It will also let you save your files in all of these formats as well as a very large number of formats for other software programs including versions of *AmiPro*, *Microsoft Word*, *OfficeWriter*, *MultiMate*, *OpenOffice* (formerly known as *WordStar*), *Professional Write*, *XyWrite*, *Quattro Pro*, *Lotus* and *Excel*. This makes it very versatile and easy to work with and a very refreshing change from Microsoft's monopolistic approach of making it tediously difficult to do it any way other than their way.

A training video comes on DVD accompanying the *WordPerfect X4 Suite* and will help new users quickly learn how to use *WordPerfect X4*. For existing users, the DVD instructional video will help them learn the new capabilities with respect to creating PDF files as well as importing such files and altering them.

At the time of writing, *WordPerfect X5* was the latest version. It has taken a major step towards improving collaborative computing. For instance, it allows users to access documents on any Microsoft *SharePoint* Server. Thus, you can review the same document with multiple people; compare versions and track changes directly from *WordPerfect X5*. An updated *iFilter* enables you to search documents on the *SharePoint* Server by using *Google Desktop Search* and *Windows Desktop Search*. You can also easily exchange documents created in the *Microsoft Office 7* suite.

This new version permits you to access information directly from the Web. For example, you could update stock share prices in a document through a simple "refresh".

There is now a tight integration with *Nuance PaperPort*, which is a high end document management program which I will discuss later. You can take scans of documents in PDF format from *PaperPort* and convert them into *WordPerfect* documents.

WordPerfect boasts of over 20 million users worldwide. It continues to be a leading product in the field of word processing and desktop publishing. I highly recommend it.

Chapter 5

Microsoft Word

A Dominant Player

When Microsoft came out with its first really commercially successful version of *Windows* known as *3.1*, it very quickly grabbed market share for its word processing software called *Word*. Microsoft quickly capitalized on its success and *Word* is now regarded as the most popular word processing software on the market.

In common with *WordPerfect*, it has a very powerful table building capability. Thus, you can delete cells and split them by right clicking on your mouse. Table cells will resize themselves according to the content that is placed within them. Within the cell of a table, it is possible to orient your text vertically. A number of fancy borders are also available and, it is possible to split a table cell diagonally.

In common with other programs in the suite, a feature shades out and hides items on pull-down menus which are not used frequently. They will, however, reappear by clicking on the arrow at the bottom of the menu. This "personalized menu" feature can be disabled by those who would rather not use it.

The program comes with a number of clip art images that can be incorporated into documents. Also included are sound files--yes, you can even include a sound file in your document! Just click on the sound file icon and your speakers will play the sound for you! So, if you have offended your boss, your other half, your parents, your kids, whoever....you can send them an electronic note with some soothing music! This feature was no longer present in *Microsoft Word 2007* and more recent versions.

A powerful editing feature allows you to change the colouring and style of any clip art or imported images and, of course, these can be sized to fit the space that you've allocated for them in your document.

A very powerful feature that was introduced with *Microsoft Word 2000* is the ability to copy multiple images for pasting. Thus, it is possible to copy up to 12 pieces of text or graphics (or whatever) and paste them into your document, either all at once or in the sequence which you desire. In addition, text files can be previewed before pasting, however, this is not the case for graphic files which are itemized as "Item 1", "Item 2", "Item 3", etc.

A very neat feature enables you to look at the document as it would appear for printing, or as it would appear when placed on the Internet as a Web page.

The view menu also allows you to magnify or reduce your page size and provides you with a preview of what the text would look like at those reduced or enlarged magnifications. This is certainly a useful feature since many times I have reduced a document, only to find that the text is illegible and I am scrambling for a more powerful pair of glasses!

When *Word 2000* was released, it introduced the ability to handle multilingual documents in English, French or Spanish and to modify the spelling and grammar checking for these languages. *Microsoft Word* has also been designed in such a way that all of its foreign language versions (with the exception of Tai, Vietnamese and Indic languages) are in one worldwide form which permits multinational companies to install one version of software around the world; thereby reducing support and training costs.

Word 2000 introduced another change. It can generate tables of contents for both printed and online documents. The table of contents for online documents can be changed to hyperlinks. Basically, these permit a user to click on a hyperlink (usually designated in a different text colour) and they will be taken directly to that topic; a very powerful feature!

With *Word 2000*, Microsoft introduced numerous new features for creating and sending text-rich e-mail and Web-ready documents. These are probably the greatest strengths of the latest versions of this software.

Microsoft introduced new features in *Versions 2002* and *2003*. In the latter, there are new page layout views. Another new feature which could be of interest to those working in a collaborative environment is the ability to lock styles so that someone who is editing a document you have carefully created does not mess the whole thing up!

One feature which I really like is the ability to compare changes made to a document (especially if you have a dual monitor). You can place one version of the document on one monitor and the other on a second and see what has changed by using a new synchronous scrolling feature–neat stuff!

Microsoft Word 2003 was a "cleaner looking" version of the 2000 edition but did not offer any new "blow your socks off" features that would make you want to rush out and purchase it. It was designed to work better in a networked collaborative environment.

Microsoft Word 2007 has a new interface which offers an entirely new "look" when you open the program. It also offers your menu in a new "ribbon style". This enables you to mouse over various styles which are applied to your entire document and lets you see what they look like before you make a choice. It also offers a number of themes for your page layout and again, applies these to your entire document and lets you see what it will look like before you select the theme.

For writers, you get a running word count which can be useful if you are preparing articles for newspapers, magazines or for descriptions in catalogues.

Microsoft Word 2007 let you create organizational charts but, in practice, I have found this feature to be quite limited in scope. On the other hand, the program offered much greater flexibility in creating bar charts, pie charts and several other styles both in two-dimensions and in 3D. You were offered a number of drawing tools, clip art, shapes, word art (fancy fonts) and a limited number of symbols.

If you are involved in desktop publishing, *Microsoft Word 2007* let you create cross-references to words within your document. This is a powerful feature.

One feature which really blew me away was the translation link to *WorldLingo* which will translate your document in a matter of minutes and send it back to you. It's free for up to 500 words at a time! Just be warned that your material is not encrypted, so you may want to take care when it comes to sending out confidential or sensitive documents.

For output, you can send to a computer printer, send documents as an e-mail attachment, fax over the Web, create PDF files, or save your documents in xml for use on the Web. When it comes to security, you can encrypt your documents, add a digital signature or restrict access.

One feature which I like is the envelope template where an envelope is already laid out for you. It's also easy to create labels and to perform mail merges.

What appears above is a brief summary of a very comprehensive word processing package which is now heavily oriented towards the electronic world. *Microsoft Word* is a leader in its field and is widely used for both business and personal use.

At the time of writing, *Word 2010* was the latest edition. It introduced some new formatting features so that you can introduce gradient fill, reflections and shadows when working with fonts. It also includes picture editing tools so you don't have to leave the program to make basic changes.

Word 2010 has taken a leaf out of Microsoft *Publisher's* book and now lets you choose from a number of themes involving the coordination of colours, fonts, styles etc., so as to create a consistent image to your customers and associates.

In *Word 2010* the file menu has changed and you're now offered a centralized place to manage your tasks and you can even customize tabs according to your needs. Finally, there is a recovery feature which lets you recover documents which you have forgotten to save–I wish they had introduced this right from the get-go!

Chapter 6

Some of the Smaller Players in Word Processing

IBM Word Pro

The word processing software by Lotus (now part of IBM) is called *Word Pro* (formerly known as *Ami Pro*). This is a fully functional word processing program with many advanced features, however, it does not enjoy the same market share as Microsoft's *Word* or Corel's *WordPerfect*.

In common with *WordPerfect*, *Word Pro* offers automatic timed backups which you can set at regular intervals which will allow you to revert to the original in case of emergencies.

One interesting feature which is available in the setup preferences is to control the number of levels of undo the level which you find most convenient.

IBM *Word Pro* contains most of the features which I discussed earlier, however, it is strongly oriented towards team work and collaborative computing with business associates. To further facilitate this collaborative computing, *Word Pro* permits users of Microsoft *Word* or Corel's *WordPerfect* to switch to menus that are similar to those with which they are already familiar. It also works with *Word* so that documents can be seamlessly exchanged.

One interesting feature of *Word Pro* is the "click here block" which enables you to indicate the location where text or data is to be inserted. This is a useful tool when editing or when creating documents that are to be assembled by a variety of different people. In addition, *Word Pro* provides the facility to manage these "click here" blocks in your document and to change their properties.

In the area of speech recognition, *Word Pro* is closely integrated with *ViaVoice*; an IBM product (now supported by ScanSoft Inc.) which I will be discussing in another chapter when I cover voice dictation.

Like its counterparts, *WordPerfect* and Microsoft *Word*, *Word Pro* also allows documents to be converted to HTML for use on the Web. It also has the capability to create hyperlinks in the document, so that a connection to that Web address can be made immediately by clicking on the link.

One very neat feature of *Word Pro* is the ease in creating headers and footers. When you click at the top or bottom of your document, the header or footer toolbar appears automatically which enables you to do the necessary formatting.

Like *Word* and *WordPerfect*, it is possible to wrap text around graphics and handles are provided to rotate and position graphics within the document. It is also possible to create watermarks--background graphics that can be applied to pages, tables, table cells, frames, headers, footers and columns. As discussed previously, this is a useful feature in the event that you want to place a watermark stating "confidential" as a layer under your text on every page of your document; thereby reminding readers to treat the material with care.

All in all, *Word Pro* is a powerful program and is closely integrated with the other members of the *IBM Lotus SmartSuite*. It is now up to release of *Version 9.8* which works on the *Windows XP* platform and with *Windows 7*.

IBM Lotus Symphony

In 2008, IBM introduced a freely downloadable office suite called *Lotus Symphony*. This rolls three applications into one application window which allows you to jump between them with ease:

1) word processing
2) presentation software
3) spreadsheet

You should be warned that *Lotus Symphony* will only import *Microsoft Office* and *OpenOffice* documents. So if you are working with *Lotus WordPro* or *Corel WordPerfect* you will have to work in *LibreOffice*.

LibreOffice

LibreOffice is an open source productivity suite that operates on Windows, Linux and Macintosh platforms. It comprises six components:

Writer: which as its name suggests is a word processing program.

Draw: which lets you make sketches and diagrams.

Calc: which is a spreadsheet program.

Impress: which is a multimedia presentation program.

Base: which is a database program

Math: which helps you work with mathematical formulas, equations, etc.

A PDF writer is common to all the elements and permits you to create your own PDF documents from any of the six components.

OpenOffice Writer

In 1999, Sun Microsystems acquired *StarOffice*, a software suite which commanded about one-third of the German office suite market. As a part of its marketing strategy, Sun Microsystems originally made the suite available to users at no cost, however, the latest version *StarOffice Writer 9* was part of the *StarOffice Suite 9*. After Oracle's purchase of Sun, the software has been re-named "*Oracle OpenOffice Writer*" and became part of the *Oracle OpenOffice Suite*. In June 2011, Oracle donated the code of *OpenOffice* to the Apache Software Foundation's incubator.

OpenOffice Writer is compatible with the file formats found in *Microsoft Office 2007* and *2010*.

OpenOffice Writer is less elaborate than *Corel WordPerfect*, *Microsoft Word* or *IBM WordPro*, all of which I discussed earlier, however, it contains most of the basic essentials for document preparation. It is compatible with *Microsoft Word* and I certainly did not experience any difficulties when I opened *Word* files. Actually, this flexibility makes this program a really valuable tool in the word processing arena.

You can also perform mail merges. In addition, you can perform a "search and replace". You can also add notes, bookmarks and add cross-references.

OpenOffice Writer permits you to insert different types of objects into your document and these can range from simple lines of text, to graphics, pictures or even complete videos! One feature which I very much like is the ability to crop pictures, place borders around them and to resize them right within the document. In addition, a reasonable selection of fonts, photographs and clip art graphics are provided with the program. Indeed, it will even let you incorporate sound and video into your documents!

The program permits you to establish styles before commencing your document.

Because *OpenOffice Writer* software is relatively straightforward and unencumbered with many of the features provided by the other programs, it is much simpler to learn. It contains excellent instructions in the Help File for creating new documents and I found that I could get up to speed very quickly.

One interesting feature is the automatic word completion which can be activated (or deactivated). In other words, it will automatically complete words of longer than five characters that have already been used in the document and this is done while you are typing.

OpenOffice Writer also comes with a spell check which can be activated to indicate errors as you are typing. A Thesaurus is also featured and the program also offers the search and replace capabilities (thus you can replace the name "Joan" by "Jill").

Simple, straightforward tables can also be created. You are provided with most of the tools you need for table design and for field properties.

Toolbar buttons enable all of the usual word processing functions to be performed, i.e., select whether you want to create a heading or body text and set your font style and size. There are bold, italic and underline buttons, together with justification settings as well as bulleting and numbering. You have all the basic formatting tools you need to handle text.

You can save your files in PDF format; complete with indexing and bookmarks. This capability on its own, makes the program a serious contender in the competitive world of word processing software.

All in all, a very powerful introductory word processing program which contains most of the features that would be required by the average user.... and at a very reasonable price!

Adobe Buzzword

Buzzword is a word processing program which was acquired by Adobe and which can be accessed on the Web for free. It only offers a limited number of fonts but does offer basic formatting such as creating headers and footers. It is great for collaboration between groups of employees since they can add comments. It's also useful if you want to produce nice looking documents online with coloured backgrounds and coloured text. Having said all this, I really would not classify *Buzzword* as a meat and potatoes word processing program for most businesses.

WordPad

WordPad is a word processing package that comes with *Windows 95, 98, 2000, ME* and *XP* operating systems and it is also present in *Vista* and *Windows 7*. It is a very rudimentary program that provides the basics for creating a document. These include the ability to select fonts, to bold, to italicise or underline text and to justify it (left, right or centre) on the page. It also contains a bulleting function. You can insert pictures, objects, create a drawing or add date and time to your document. A colour palette enables you to colour text. Documents can be saved to disk or printed out. *WordPad* provides the barest of bare essentials to do your word processing and that's about it!

Chapter 7

The Role of Colour in Offset
and Digital Printing

A Brief Word About Colour

Very frequently, desktop publishing involves the use of colour. I'll provide a brief description of the terms which are used, as follows.

RGB: which stands for Red-Green-Blue and is the colour you see on your computer monitor.

CMYK: stands for Cyan-Magenta-Yellow-Black (the "K" standing for black) and these are the four "process" colours used in full-colour offset printing by commercial printing houses. It is also used by colour laser computer printers as well as colour photocopiers, both of which feature four colour toner cartridges; one for each of the process colours. In essence, the print job is passed through the printer or copier in such a way that each of these CMYK colours can be applied one at a time to produce a "colour photograph-like" picture.

Often, it is a challenge to match the RGB colour you see on your monitor with the CMYK colour; so don't be surprised if they look different. The good news is that Apple has filed a patent for a new kind of monitor that uses adjustable filters to display CMYK, but I have no idea when it will be available.

Spot Colour: refers to applying two or more colours separately in such a way that they do not overlap one another to produce another colour. Usually, the colours are defined by using a Pantone swatch which enables a commercial printer to duplicate that colour when mixing inks. Care should be taken since most spot colours can appear different on glossy as opposed to mat paper stock.

If you are using spot colour, say a small red area on a text which is largely printed in black, you will need to present your commercial printer with two black and white images; one representing the black colour which your commercial printer will print using black ink and the other one representing the red colour which your commercial printer will print in red ink. A few desktop publishing programs will enable you to do this separation.

Some of the more sophisticated programs such as *Adobe Photoshop* will let you do the full CMYK separations for full colour printing. This is a very powerful feature which makes the production of colour documents much easier than was the case in the past.

Indeed, many printing houses use this product for colour separation and to make the film that is used to create printing plates. For example, for a "full colour" job (CMYK), it will create the plates for the three basic colours plus black.

Offset Printing

Offset printing is a method of mass producing documents, books, pamphlets, etc. in which the images are transferred to paper through the use of metal or paper plates.

In the case of printing in black (being provided by the ink) and white (being the paper) your commercial printer would use one plate. Now, your printer can achieve various shades of grey since these are just black ink that is not applied so "thickly". This is achieved by the density of dots of ink on the plate.

Printing with "spot colours" usually involves two (or more) colours simultaneously. Some older AB Dick offset printing machines will print two colours; one right after the other but in such a way that the colours do not overlap. Alternatively, the sheets can be fed twice through a single colour machine with great care being taken to make sure the alignment of the second colour is as near to perfect as possible. Different shades of each colour can be achieved by applying less ink (in dots). Thus, you could have a deep red, medium red, pale red all produced by the same plate. The same for blue or any other colour.

On the other hand if you are going for full process CMYK colour, the downside is that the offset presses can be quite expensive because of the technology and equipment involved and very short print runs can be prohibitively expensive. The good news is that new technology is replacing some of these mammoth CMYK printing presses; especially for shorter print runs.

Digital Printing

Probably the best way to describe digital printing is by way of an illustration.

When I send a book to my commercial printer, I can create a high quality PDF file and he inserts it into his personal computer which then transmits it to a Cannon digital photocopier which prints the number of copies he has specified–all collated and double-sided (or as specified). The PDF file which I supply, could have been burned onto a CD-ROM, DVD or I can transmit it as an attachment to an e-mail over the Web.

The same thing applies when I need a book cover. I send him a ffle and he can print in black and white, spot colours or in full colour (CMYK) on light card stock.

This is great technology and a quantum leap from the labourious task of setting lead type and using a printing drum to create the pages–a process which was widely used until about 50 years ago. (Remember the old Gutenberg press and the versions of it which dominated the world of the printing market since the 15th Century up until late last Century?)

In this era, the photocopier and the computer printer have merged into one machine. And, that's not all. Some of these machines will staple documents and I have even seen one which will perform bookbinding for you. The bad news is that such equipment will empty your cash piggy bank fairly quickly! They are not inexpensive; even on a leased basis.

Chapter 8

Creating Portable Documents

Adobe Acrobat

Adobe Acrobat enables you to convert documents into what is known as a "Portable Document Format" or PDF file which I discussed previously. Once converted, these documents can be transmitted electronically as e-mail attachments or be made available for download from a Web site. The original appearance of the document is preserved. In order to view a PDF document, you will need to install a copy of *Acrobat Reader*, which is available as a free download from Adobe's Web site. As a consequence, many Web sites feature documents in PDF format that can be downloaded. This is particularly the case for annual reports for public companies, instructional material, sales material....indeed anything that has to look better than the plain text that is so typical of most e-mail messages.

This program is essential if you want to create reliable and secure documents. It will be a boon if you are a lawyer, accountant or other professional, or if you are involved with publishing. It has also become a standard in the field of commercial printing.

Adobe Acrobat 9 is available in three different flavours: *Standard* for regular folks, *Pro* for preparing material for commercial printing and ideal for small business and *Pro Extended* which will appeal to those who have to make presentations using *Flash* and 3D images or for those using Computer Aided Design (CAD).

The following comments are based on my review of the *Pro* version.

One feature I really like about *Adobe Acrobat 9 Pro* is the very clean layout on the opening page, where icons on the taskbar let you select what you want to do. Thus, you can create a PDF document; combine documents; collaborate with others; add comments to a document or digitally sign it; create a form or add multimedia. Most important of all, you are offered a number of security features to apply to your document. I'll briefly review each of them in turn.

Create a PDF File: can usually be done in the application you are working in such as *Microsoft Word* or *WordPerfect X4*. *Acrobat* will preserve your original layouts, fonts, colours and images. In spite of this, images which appear in print form often have a different appearance when they appear on your monitor, so *Adobe Acrobat* permits you to "tweak" them so that they will look their best after being electronically transmitted. Another nifty new way of creating a PDF text file is to save a blank page in PDF format in *Microsoft Word* and then open it in *Acrobat 9*. You can then use the text editor to add text! I tried the same trick with *WordPerfect X4* but it did not work, since it would not permit me to save a blank page in PDF format. (Maybe in the next version?) You can also add PDF images from a scanner.

Create a PDF Portfolio: enables you to combine a number of separate files created in different programs into one portfolio. This could include multimedia files. You can add a header and background colour and choose from four basic layout schemes. You can even add a welcome page! Once your portfolio has been created, you can edit each of your files independently of one another. Probably one of the best features is that you can attach your portfolio to an e-mail and you can even secure it with a password.

Combine Files: lets you combine files and create a single PDF. For example, you could add a JPEG graphics image file. If there is a problem, the program will instruct you to remove the file.

PDF Optimizer: to reduce PDF file sizes. This is especially useful if you are dealing with very large documents which may cause problems at the mail server level if you are sending your documents as e-mail attachments.

OCR Text Recognition: can be used to convert a PDF document into editable text.

Collaborate: if the person you are working with also has *Adobe Acrobat 9 Pro* installed, you can collaborate live with them by sharing page views by means of a live chat session using *Acrobat.com.*

Add Highlights and Comments: allows you to highlight, underline or cross out text and add comments to a PDF document without changing the original. You can also mark things up with a pen tool or add arrows and shapes. If you want to replace text, you can select the word or words and write over them. They will be added to your list of comments. If you are set up with a microphone, you can add voice comments. You can also add comments that appear at the bottom of a document or be inserted as "Sticky Notes" at a specific location. Comments can be made by different people reviewing a document and be sorted according to the reviewer. The program also enables you to create an e-mail with the comments of reviewers.

Searching a Document: using the search window or the "find toolbar", you can search a PDF document or portfolio for a certain word or phrase.

Sign a Document: lets you add your digital signature if you already have one. If you do not, you can create one. This is password protected and is a really neat feature.

Security Features: permit you to encrypt your PDF document either with a certificate or a password, however, you cannot perform this function if your document has already been digitally signed. Security features let you control access to a document; set permissions as to who can save, copy, print or modify it. This is very important if you are involved with copyrighted materials as well as for controlling access to sensitive or confidential documents. In this regard, it should be noted that you also have access to a "blackout" tool to hide sensitive areas of a document that you do not want the recipient to see. If you require a higher level of security, documents can be encrypted.

Create a Form: with *Adobe Acrobat 9* you can create a form in one of three ways: either by scanning an existing paper form; using an existing form which you have created in *Microsoft Word* or *Excel*. You can also start from scratch, designing it yourself or using an Adobe template. Templates have already been created for a variety of uses such as to create an order form, quotation, purchase order, expense account, employment application; to name a few. If you can adopt one of theses templates, it will save you a lot of time. The form you have created could be accessed over the Internet and if saved as a dynamic PDF, it can be filled out by the recipient and transmitted back when completed. This revolutionizes the form-filling process with the added bonus that the boxes in the form can be read when it is sent back since they are typed rather than scratched in with a pen! Once forms have been returned, you can compile the data from the form in an *Excel* spreadsheet, where it can be analysed. Wow! The form business has really evolved!

MultiMedia: you can embed audio files, videos and multimedia in PDF documents.

Saving Your Files: in a number of different formats, such as PDF/A which is suitable for files imported into a *Microsoft Word* document for transmission by e-mail, for archiving, search and retrieval at a later stage, etc. You can also save in the PDF/X file format which is designed for graphics professionals and is widely accepted as a standard in the commercial printing industry; because it saves files in their highest resolution. Essentially, *Acrobat Distiller*, which is a component of this program, lets you define the setting for your document such as "Standard", "Press Quality", "Smallest File Size", "PDF/A" or "PDF/X".

Print Production Tools and "Pre-Flight": consists of a sophisticated set of tools to prepare PDF files for commercial printers including colour conversion, hairlines and crop marks. In addition, you can perform a "pre-flight" test which will conduct over 400 checks for output errors. These features will be invaluable if you are involved in preparing catalogues, advertising or any other material for commercial printing.

Acrobat 10: was available at the time of writing. *Acrobat 10* and is also referred to as *Acrobat X*. It has further developed the concept of the "portfolio" that was previously available to combine PDF files. Now you can incorporate Adobe *Flash* video, other video and Microsoft Office files. It has also become easier to create interactive forms. Other features facilitate annotations, comments and marking tools to help with collaboration between colleagues.

If you have upgraded from *Version 9* to *X*, you will immediately notice that the interface (GUI) has changed. No longer are there 12 pull-down menus...but six. You can now more easily export full files or portions of them to Microsoft *Word* or an *Excel* spreadsheet where they can be edited. (In fairness, Version 9 allowed you to export to *Word* but it wasn't a feature that worked very well).

All-in-all, Acrobat is still one of the best ways to get your print jobs into the hands of your commercial printer. It remains the best for retaining document features across different platforms and for use on the Internet. For example, I created an order form in Microsoft *Word*; converted it into a PDF and posted it on our Web site. Customers can download it and it retains the original appearance of the *Word* document; regardless of whether they are using a PC or a Mac. It also remains a champion in the form filling process and is great for collaborative work in a business environment. The security features are to be commended. In short....definitely a program that should be used by every small business.

ABBYY PDF Transformer

The *ABBYY PDF Transformer* is a software package with three basic functions. It will help you convert any type of PDF file into a form that can be edited and it will also retain the original layout and formatting. It also works in reverse, allowing you to take any document created in *Microsoft Word* or *Microsoft Excel* and create a PDF with it. The software also lets you modify documents e.g., you can add stamps. It also provides a redaction tool which enables you to remove sensitive information or to remove unwanted text or pictures.

This software lets you combine multiple files into one PDF document, or you can convert only a part of a document. You can restrict access to your PDF documents if you want.

Once you have converted documents to PDF, they can be sent as e-mail attachments. You can save in high quality to send to a commercial printer.

You can also save to disc for archiving and searching. This is made easier by adding a "Bates stamp" which gives each document a number, a date and indicates how many pages the document contains.

ABBYY PDF Transformer 3 is built around ABBYY's Adaptive Document Recognition Technology (ADRT). This treats the document as a whole, rather than as individual pages. By taking this approach, the software is able to preserve the logical organization of a document such as columns and tables. It will also recognize fonts, headers, footnotes, etc.

If you are involved in any serious way in working with, and managing PDF documents, you will find this program very useful. Also, it will appeal to those who are looking for a much less expensive alternative to *Adobe Acrobat*, since it sells for about one-quarter to one-fifth of the price.

Embedding Fonts with PDF Documents

I should add one warning about PDF files. If you send a PDF file which contains a font that is not one of the "plain vanilla font styles", *Adobe Reader* will substitute a font. That's fine and dandy when the substituted font is similar in appearance, but this is not always the case and you could end up with something that looks very different from the original.

In such instances, you will want to use the *Acrobat Distiller* to embed definitions of the fonts which you are using in your PDF file. If you want to make sure that your document will appear **exactly** as you created it, then set the subsetting in *Distiller* to 100%.

Chapter 9

The "Soup to Nuts" Publishing Programs

PagePlus

PagePlus is a relatively inexpensive desktop publishing program published by Serif. In many ways, it competes with *Microsoft Publisher* (see below) but it does enable you to send your work to a commercial printer in PDF format. Having said that, it does not compete with some of the higher end products which I will cover later, such as Corel's *Ventura*, *FrameMaker*, *QuarkXPress* or *Adobe inDesign*.

One thing I like about the program is that it offers a wizard to guide you through various projects such as:

- business cards
- business stationery
- brochures
- newsletters
- flyers
- calendars
- gifts

- fun
- greeting cards
- invitations
- posters
- postcards
- certificates
- Web sites

Of course, you can always start from scratch or open an existing publication.

The program is supported by a number of tutorials which are designed to help both beginners as well as experienced users. For example, these cover the basics of importing images and introduce you to a number of layout aids plus the mechanics of using text frames.

Unlike other desktop publishing programs, this one has a very strong support for graphics which includes some of the more sophisticated features that you would normally find in a graphics program, such as gradient and bitmap fills. It also lets you create curved lines and you can wrap text around graphics on your page.

Interestingly enough, the program will let you work in tables and provides you with the basic tools for formatting them.

The program also offers you a way to create a Web page which you can use to customize according to your needs, however, this is not a full-blown Web publishing program but it will give you some rudimentary material which you can incorporate into any Web site. When I say "rudimentary" I do not mean to imply that the material does not look "professional" but you don't get all the bells and whistles which you need to publish a full-blown Web site.

A resource CD-ROM accompanies this program and this will help you learn how to publish in PDF format.

Another resource on the CD-ROM will help to build a book using a built-in "book manager". This includes creating a table of contents and building an index. Your final project can then be saved in PDF format and taken to a commercial printer or published on the Web.

The resource CD-ROM will also show you how to set up an auction catalogue as well as a photo album. One interesting project that you can perform with this software is to create sequentially numbered tickets for use at an event or for a draw.

As I mentioned above, the program can be used to create greeting cards and the resource CD-ROM will show you how to create a set of mail merged address labels which can be very useful for sending out Christmas cards or for invitations to special events.

All in all, this is a great little application if you need a simple, inexpensive, yet easy-to-use desktop publishing program.

Version 11 lets you import and edit PDF documents which was a welcome new feature.

At the time of writing, *PagePlus Essentials X4* was the latest version. It has a sticker price of under $50 US and features 550 professionally-designed templates and a 1,000 piece on-screen gallery of illustrations, symbols and silhouettes. It provides drawing tools and even a built in "PhotoLab" to fix up your pictures.

Microsoft Publisher

Microsoft Publisher is a superb introductory publishing package which makes the task of preparing numerous types of documents very simple by providing a very large number of professionally designed templates. These can be customized to your particular requirements.

The templates in *Microsoft Publisher 2007* cover the following: categories:

- advertisements
- award certificates
- banners

- brochures
- business cards
- business forms

- calendars
- catalogues
- e-mail
- flyers
- gift certificates
- greeting cards
- invitation cards
- labels
- letterhead
- menus
- newsletters
- paper folding projects
- postcards
- programs for religious services, music or theatre
- quick publication covers
- resumés
- signs
- Web site layout designs in html which you can publish to the Web
- with compliments cards

Each of these categories feature numerous different templates which you can adapt to your particular needs. You can also download a number of additional templates online.

It will let you import documents from *Microsoft Word*. You can create tables; you can group items so they stay together, and you are offered ruler guides and layout guides. You can also perform mail, e-mail and catalogue merge using Business Contact Manager. Actually, this can help you personalize your e-mail messages and e-mail newsletters, which is a great way of staying in touch with customers, clients, shareholders or employees.

You can save your publications in PDF format. *Office Publisher 2007* will even alert you to possible design errors before your job is sent to a commercial printer. The program provides full support in the form of 4-colour (CMYK) separations and the ability to handle spot colour. (See earlier discussion.)

The previous 2003 version introduced the concept of "Design Sets" which apply a common theme and colour combination over various different items such as business cards, letterhead, envelopes, labels, etc. In this way, your business can convey a uniform look to those outside, rather than a hotchpotch of different appearances. On the other hand, some of these can be achieved by using special pre-printed paper and envelope sets which you can purchase from many stationary supply stores.

In addition to the pre-prepared templates, you can start with a blank piece of paper or card. You can choose from a variety of fold styles to create brochures, tent cards, postcards, business cards, greeting cards, etc.

You can also send output to the Web and the *Microsoft Publisher* enables you to establish hyperlinks and provides navigation bars to enable people to move around inside your document on the Web. The software also lets you create online forms and even contains a number of animated pictures in its gallery which you can use in Web publications.

The templates are made out in a series of frames, which you can customize according to your needs. An "AutoFit" feature lets you fit text created within a specific frame.

Publisher is closely integrated with the *Microsoft Office Suite* and has much the same feel as other software products in the suite. It also features background spell checking and auto correct.

Publisher really came of age when the 2000 version was released. Since then, it has been further improved with the 2002, 2003 and 2007 versions. Thus, you can merge data from a Microsoft *Access* database or an *Excel* spreadsheet file into a publication. This is a great feature if you are involved with preparing catalogues.

When *Publisher* was first released, it was oriented towards the home user. Since then, Microsoft has oriented it more and more towards the small business market and improved its features for commercial printing, however (rightly or wrongly), it still appears to be regarded with some distain by commercial printers. Having said that, it is ideal for projects if you are using a colour inkjet or colour laser printer. The cost of these has dramatically fallen in recent years but when using them you still have to be on guard for the cost of your consumables, i.e., inkjet and toner cartridges.

At the time of writing, *Publisher 2010* was the latest; either as a stand-alone version or part of *Microsoft Office Professional 2010*. Strangely enough, it does not feature the "ribbons" of other members of the suite and has instead, retained the *Windows 7* toolbar at the top.

This new version features "Building Blocks" which provide you with a number of options to enable you to pull together a number of separate elements in order to create a good looking document in a relatively short space of time.

Many features and functions of the program are easily located in the "Backstage View"; a new feature which distinguishes this version from earlier ones. Here you will find functions such as "print" or "share". It does not feature the things that you do to your document such as formatting, writing or editing.

A "Design Checker" lets you check the information for commercial printing. Obviously, Microsoft has taken the criticism of commercial printers to heart!

The Print Shop

The Print Shop Deluxe is published by Broderbund and is now in Version 23. It is a very extensive home and business graphics software package. When I looked at it several years ago, it comprised a total of eight CD-ROMs; six of which contained supporting clip art. It is now published on a DVD. You also get over 20,000 graphics and images. In addition, you also get 1,000 ready-made templates for your projects and over 850 different styles of fonts.

This software is ideal if you are preparing letterheads, cards and flyers as well as for making signs, banners, etc. Wizards are available to guide you through the process and output can be saved or exported in PDF format, for professional printing or to maintain the original document appearance in different media formats, such as print-on-paper or the Web. It also enables you to do photo editing. You can save your files in JPEG, PDF, TIFF and other formats. It also features a set of "Dynamic Search Tools".

Earlier versions came with a superb user's manual which was well laid out and contained many illustrations. Unfortunately, the manual is no longer available with this version. Also, in earlier versions, there were two graphic reference books; one on the clip art (*ClikArt®*) and another which contained the images of backdrops, borders, numerous graphics, photos and fine art that were contained on the CD-ROMs.

The introductory screen offered you multiple project choices. In an earlier version which I reviewed, they were as follows:

- greeting cards
- signs
- pamphlets
- booklets

- photo pages
- letterhead
- business cards
- envelopes
- calendars
- postcards
- CD/DVD labels
- online greetings

- certificates
- mailing labels
- invitations
- photo greeting cards
- newsletters
- skins for iPods
- photo book pages
- family trees

It provided you with 6-month access to an online product known as *Million Image Club.*

The first step in using this software is to select your project and choose from a very large number of layouts or start from scratch, using the designer guidance which is provided in the package.

The second step is to work on your creations by adding graphics from the clip art collections contained on the DVD or by importing your own graphics or photos. Step-by-step instructions are provided that make this task extremely easy. You can edit photos, touch them up or convert them to special effects.

The third step is to output the work that you have created; either to your computer printer, for posting on the Web or by e-mail.

Care should be taken when using this product to observe copyright laws. Thus, most of the clip art can be used for home projects but the inclusion of graphic images on products for sale is specifically prohibited. I would advise you to carefully read the documentation that comes with this product to make sure that you are not leaving yourself open to legal action.

In addition to the *DeLuxe Version*, there is a *Pro Publisher DeLuxe Version* with even more features. If you want something less expensive, there is also a *Standard Version* with fewer features!

Small Business Publisher

Small Business Publisher by Belltech Systems will help you in printing labels, letterhead, flyers, name badges, postcards and envelopes. It provides you with ready-made templates as well as many graphics. You can also import your own graphics. In addition, it has a number of design tools to create shapes or professional designs.

The latest *Version 5.1* will work under the *Windows 7* operating system.

In summary, it is a fairly basic publishing system good for creating advertisements, brochures, labels, business card, etc.

Chapter 10

The Heavyweights of Desktop Publishing

Corel Ventura

Corel Ventura is an ideal product for use in creating long and structured documents.

When you open *Corel Ventura* for the first time, you'll notice that it contains more toolbars than the average application. These can be docked to various sides of the screen or they can be left floating. The toolbars can also be customized to accommodate the manner in which you work. *Corel Ventura* is created around the basic concept that each document you produce, whether it be a single page sheet or a multi-page manual; consists of three elements.

1.   The style sheet which contains all the tags and master pages that are used in your document. The tags allow you to automate changes in your publication and help to produce a uniform appearance. Tags permit you to change the appearance of a long document e.g., before the headings in the document have been tagged you can change the font style once and have this applied to all the headings within your document, without having to visit each heading individually in order to make the change.

     Tags cover four areas:

     a) paragraphs
     b) characters

    c) frame tags

    d) border tags (which are used in tables).

2.   The master page which allows you to establish and design the elements in a chapter such as the page size, orientation, margins, backgrounds, headers and footers, etc. Essentially, they are the templates for your page layout.

3.   The chapter(s) can contain text or graphics. Every *Corel Ventura* publication must have a minimum of one chapter. As in a book, you can divide chapters into manageable sections. Chapters can also contain multiple master pages.

A "publication manager" can be found in the *Ventura* navigator and this permits you to look at the style sheets, master pages and chapters in your publication. The publication manager also allows you to examine the structure of your table of contents and to manage indexes and cross-references.

Text or graphics and pictures are contained in "frames". These can be positioned on a page according to your requirements and can be "anchored" so that there will always remain with a specific piece of text on a specific page.

A library is provided to store commonly used items so that they can be quickly accessed for use when creating new documents. Libraries are also helpful in a workgroup environment, since they will permit different members of the group to access items which are common to all or most of them.

As you might expect, *Corel Ventura* is capable of producing colour separations, ready for commercial printing. It is also ideal for handling long documents and creating tables of contents, indexes, footnotes and cross-references. When creating Web documents, you can hyperlink them.

You can also create tables in *Ventura* and you can perform some mathematical calculations, as in spreadsheets.

You can create HTML pages for use on the Web. In addition, *Corel Barista* can be used to create *Java Powered* documents, which gives you more control over them than standard HTML. The documents created in this manner can be moved across platforms with any *Java Compatible* browser.

Corel Ventura comes with an extensive selection of clip art and the user manual is well laid out and relatively easy to read. In addition, the software comes with a number of tutorials designed to get you started. Personally, I found that my monitor became very cluttered when trying to view these tutorials at the same time as working in the program and this is where the use of a second monitor can be a great benefit for those who are using *Windows 98*, *Windows ME*, *Windows XP*, *Vista* or *Windows 7*--simply move the tutorial window over to the second monitor and this allows you to work on the program unencumbered! (N.B: you cannot use two monitors with *Windows 95*.)

When version 8 of *Ventura* was released, it included some new utilities for optical character recognition (OCR) and for importing scanned documents. (More about this in a later chapter.) It now includes plug-in filters that can be used with images created in Adobe *Photoshop*.

Ventura 8 was more tightly integrated with other Corel products; especially *Photo-Paint*. It also included enhancements if you wish to publish your work on the Internet.

Corel Ventura 8 came bundled with *WordPerfect 8* and Corel *PhotoPaint*. In addition, it is packaged with 40,000 clipart images together with the choice of over 1,000 fonts.

Corel Ventura 10 is the version which was available at the time of writing. A strong new feature lets you publish in Portable Document Format (PDF) which is very useful to maintain the appearance of a document when it is made available on the Web or certain mobile devices. If you want to send files to a commercial printer, you can output images in grey-scale, RGB or CMYK and files can now include crop marks, registration marks, calibration bars and file information.

Corel Ventura 10 permits you to touch up bitmap images with 50 new effects. You can share files with other programs such as *Microsoft Word*, *WordPerfect*, *Illustrator*, *Photoshop*, *Micrographx Designer*, *iGrafx designer*, Corel *Photopaint* and *Corel Designer*.

FrameMaker

FrameMaker by Adobe, gives you very strong control (by using tags) over different levels of headings and over blocks of text, thereby enabling you to readily change the appearance of an entire document. It also enables you to output your work in different formats. Thus, if you have a long, thousand-page book that you want to split up into a number of shorter booklets, it is possible to generate those shorter booklets very quickly while maintaining the integrity of cross-referencing and indexing.

Indeed, one of the biggest strengths of *FrameMaker* is its ability to handle large documents and enable you to output them in a number of different print formats, or in HTML for publishing on the Web. It is ideally suited for combining text and images. In many ways, Adobe *FrameMaker* is like having a number of publishing packages rolled into one. Thus, it can behave as a word processor; as a page layout software tool and it also handles graphics and colour.

FrameMaker's formatting layout tools enable you to change the appearance of a long document very quickly. This is achieved by changing header styles and paragraph styles which can then be applied to an entire document. You can also place your text around graphics in different ways (such as wrapping it around an image). You can organize your page layouts so that they are attractive and are consistent throughout the length of your document.

One of the biggest advantages of this program is the ability to cross-reference within the document that you're working on and also between different documents. This cross-referencing ability is very flexible and also dynamic. Thus, if you have a long document, let's say 20 chapters in length and you have a cross-reference in Chapter 1 to something that appears in Chapter 20; and you then decide to have an abridged 10 chapter version of this document with the same cross-reference that will appear in the first and last chapters, *FrameMaker* will change the cross-reference mentioned in Chapter 1 to Chapter 10 automatically.

These links which you have created in your cross-references will be automatically converted into hypertext when you use *FrameMaker* to convert your document into HTML for publication on the Web.

This software will automatically number pages for you. *FrameMaker* will also help you to create your table of contents, your index and a glossary for your document. It will also automatically generate numbering for tables, footnotes, illustrations and other elements in your document which require numbers.

Another interesting feature is the ability of *FrameMaker* to generate complex tables and sort data alphabetically or numerically within those tables. In turn, you can export tables to other applications.

Another feature of this product is that it gives you the ability to import text and graphics from other applications such as *WordPerfect* or *Microsoft Word*. You can import graphics or text by dragging and dropping. You can also work in *FrameMaker* on different platforms such as Unix or Mac and this will be of interest if you have a business in which employees are using different platforms in their workgroups.

Over 30 different pre-prepared templates are available to help you with the layout of your document. You can also create your own template styles which will allow you to define the fonts, sizes and styles of your paragraphs and headings. In addition, you can import page layouts together with the colour scheme that you have created in other applications. In the event that you want to change the formatting of your pages, you can readily achieve this by changing the layout of your master page.

You can also create both landscape and portrait page styles in the same document. (In fairness, both *WordPerfect* and *Microsoft Word* will also let you do this.) If you are using multiple columns in your document, you can straddle headlines, footers, graphics and tables across columns.

As with most word processing programs, *FrameMaker* provides you with a large dictionary so that you can perform spell checking. Those who work in foreign languages will be interested to know that 17 different foreign dictionaries are available.

Adobe has brought the power of its graphics programs to this package and you can manipulate different graphic objects, outline them or layer them. In addition, Adobe provides a number of colour models which can be very useful if you have to send your output to a commercial printer. Thus, you can create your documents with colours which are defined in Pantone so that your commercial printer can match them precisely. In addition, you can also use colour tints in your document which can be very useful in instances where your commercial printing output is in only two spot colours, as I discussed earlier, and you want to achieve the effect of more colours through the use of tints.

Version 7.1 included new filters to import files from *QuarkXPress* and Adobe *Pagemaker* (both of which will be covered later). It also permits images to be directly placed from Adobe *Photoshop*. You can also output files for print, PDF, HTML, XML and SGML. The publishing power, collaboration features and authoring tools have all been enhanced.

Version 8 lets you perform 3D modelling as well as video, audio and screen shots and is very tightly integrated with *RoboHelp 7*, if purchased in combination with that product (see review below).

Without question, Adobe *FrameMaker* is the leading desktop publishing software product for authoring long documents, however, you may still wish to use a traditional word processing program, such as *Microsoft Word* or *WordPerfect* together with a spreadsheet program, such as *Excel* to create your original material and then import it to *FrameMaker*. The advantage of taking this approach is that you can use the rich features which these word processing and spreadsheet programs offer. In addition, if you are working in a collaborative environment, the other people who are contributing material to the project can create their contributions in programs that they are likely to be familiar with, which means that they don't have to learn how to use *FrameMaker*.

Some new features were added to *FrameMaker 9* and included a new user interface and an integrated toolset. It was also improved to support the production of books and rich media content.

At the time of writing *FrameMaker 10* was the latest version. This is a high-end publishing product which enables publication of highly structured or unstructured documents in a number of different formats such as PDF, HTML and others by using an Adobe *FrameMaker Server*. Just to take a few examples, you can create glossaries of terms used in a document; you can cross-reference terms; you can create an index. All of these are great features when working on technical documents e.g., for aircraft design, pharmaceutical drug research etc.

RoboHelp

RoboHelp is a "help authoring tool" which was acquired by Adobe when it purchased Macromedia. *Version 7* has since been tightly integrated with *FrameMaker 8*. Basically, *RoboHelp* allows you to import documents which you have created in *FrameMaker* and it will do all the conversion for you to enable you to publish the material on the Web. For example, it will preserve your indexes, glossary and table of contents. It will also allow you to tweak these since cross references such as "see page number" are not relevant to material shown on the Web and such references have to be replaced with a link. Having said all that, the "integration" is a one-way street from *FrameMaker 8* to *RoboHelp* and not a two-way street. Thus, many of the changes which you make in *RoboHelp* cannot be transferred back to *FrameMaker 8* since it may not be able to incorporate them.

RoboHelp lets you change fonts and colours to enhance the Web experience. Again, you can incorporate video, digital pictures, 3D images and sound from your *FrameMaker* document. You can also preserve any animation associated with your 3D images.

RoboHelp creates your Web content in HTML so you can add a "welcome page" as well as other material not contained in your original *FrameMaker* document. The downside is that *RoboHelp* does not support XML which appears to be the direction for the future.

This software, when used in conjunction with *FrameMaker 8* could be very helpful for those in the engineering, scientific, medical and other fields which have long documents. It definitely assists in moving such material to the Web and to create user-friendly documents. One thing which I really like is the search and highlight feature which when used online will search through a long text and place a yellow highlight on the answer to your query.

At the time of writing, *RoboHelp 9* was available. It has been more tightly integrated with *FrameMaker* and permits you to distribute your content to e-book readers, mobile devices and tablets. In other words, it helps facilitate multi-channel publishing. It also lets you work collaboratively on the same documents with other colleagues who may be located far across the globe. In fairness, Microsoft *SharePoint* will let you do the same thing.

MadCap Flare

MadCap Flare basically offers much of the same functionality as *RoboHelp*, insofar as it can also be classified as "help authoring software", however, it is based on

XML rather than HTML which was one of the shortcomings of *RoboHelp*. I did not get a chance to review it but the company's Web site claims that it is a replacement for *RoboHelp*. I'll leave you to be the judge of that!

Chapter 11

The Leaders in Design and Layout

Adobe InDesign

Adobe InDesign is a design and layout program which allows you to publish to multiple media channels. It provides a tight integration between four of Adobe's programs: *Illustrato*r, *Photoshop*, *Acrobat* and *inCopy*. It competes with *QuarkXPress* (see below). It has basically replaced one of Adobe's other products: *PageMaker* which is no longer supported by Adobe.

One way of describing it is to think of it as a closet where you can "hang" the different elements that make up your page. You can anchor items on a page or link items so that they will move together, if you decide to reposition them. For example, you might want the caption under a photograph to accompany that photo to wherever it is moved. The program also features an "Align to Spine" feature which, as its name implies, automatically aligns objects that you move to the spine.

This is a great program if you are involved with the layout of magazine or newsletter pages, as well as brochures. You can use it to create book covers and posters. If you do not have a high volume of such work, you can burn your file onto a CD-ROM or a DVD and take it to a commercial printer. There, your work can be used for colour offset printing or to make prints or posters on a colour laser printer or colour laser copier.

All available typefaces are displayed in a font menu and you can perform kerning as well as margin alignment directly from within the program.

InDesign CS2 and *Version CS3* lets you work with layers which you have created in *Photoshop* directly, without having to go back to *Photoshop*. Similarly, you can re-edit a PDF document without having to go back to *Acrobat* to re-edit it. Without leaving the program, you can also create and edit drop-shadows, create feathering effects, opacity and blend modes.

The program allows you to store elements of your design as "snippets" and keep them organized in *AdobeBridge* (see later in this chapter), so that you can access them whenever they are required. It works hand-in-hand with *AdobeBridge*.

Another feature which I really like are quite a large number of pre-prepared templates. Thus, you can select from 25 layouts for brochures and adapt them to your requirements.

Adobe InDesign CS2 was created for collaboration if you have team members who are involved in a project. It also permited you to export files using PDF-X which is now used widely in the print industry for file exchange.

The more recent *InDesign CS3* will let you insert a movie into a PDF file and so long as it is embedded, it can be replayed, normally at a resolution of 72 dpi, however the "poster" which activates the movie when a mouse is passed over it can be saved at a higher resolution.

Using *InDesign CS3*, you can create a database type of PDF which can be populated with data. Any overflow can be extended on to additional pages. You can create your own tables using *InDesign CS3* or you can import them from *Microsoft Word* or *Excel*.

InDesign CS3 features a full set of controls for bulleting, numbering, kerning, margin alignment; text wrapping around graphics or other objects; to name but a few. It also lets you export your work in XHTML. It can be further edited in another program for Web authoring called *Dreamweaver* which is also published by Adobe.

InDesign CS3 certainly represents an advance in page layout, especially suited for long documents containing a lot of graphics and photos. I find that it gets over many of the shortcomings of the earlier versions of *QuarkXPress* and I am very impressed with its tight integration with other Adobe products; namely *Illustrator*, *Photoshop*, *Acrobat and inCopy*.

InDesign CS4 software lets you conduct a "preflight" to help you detect errors in your layout much quicker than in the previous *CS3* version.

CS5 boasted some enhanced productivity tools as well as allowing the import of MP3 Audio and *Flash* FLVF-4V video. It offered some new text handling tools as well as a number of panels for use when you are working on rich interactive documents. It also features document installed fonts so you don't have to attach these separately when sending output to a commercial printer. In this regard, another new feature has PDF export working in the background.

At the time of writing, the latest version was *CS5.5*. I upgraded to it in order to facilitate the conversion of books into the ePub free flowing format which is rapidly developing into a leader for the delivery of eBooks to a wide variety of portable devices such as tablets and phones. The conversion is relatively straightforward but you'll have to be aware that graphic images and tables have to be anchored to the preceding paragraph. (I'll cover this topic in more detail in *eBook Publishing for Beginners: How to Make Money Selling Your Digital Books Online* by www.Learn2succeed.com).

InDesign CS5.5 is a very useful program for creating print-on-paper books as well as the PDF versions. It features a very structured layout environment which will also be useful if you are involved with publishing newsletters, magazines or newspapers. It could also be useful in laying out the copy for advertisements. Having said all this, the program has a learning curve which may take you a little time to get up to speed. Also, I personally find that the "Help" files are not that helpful since there is no A-Z topic list.

Adobe inCopy

Adobe inCopy helps facilitate your publishing workflow and should not be confused with *Adobe inDesign* even though it is closely integrated with it. Essentially, *inCopy* will help you assemble all the elements for commercial print jobs and permits different people to work on different components.

It allows a collaboration between the copywriters, the graphic designers and the editors and features a permissions system to make sure that only certain people get access to certain files at any one time. It also keeps track of who has taken files out and who is working on them. It prevents two people working on the same file at the same time which could create a conflict when the file is saved. It also allocates files to certain people so that others cannot alter them, however, they have access to see what they look like. In other words, they can "look over the fence but not enter".

inCopy allows the creative team to look at the way a document will appear when it is in print. Thus, you get to see all the copy and whether it fits the allocated space. Similarly, it will allow writers to fill in the columns for a newspaper, magazine or newsletter. It will also give you the word count etc.

In the review mode, you can use *inCopy* to view the entire project you are working on. This is something which you cannot do in *inDesign*. You can add notes and review it in a collaborative way; make suggestions for changes or improvements without actually changing the original. This is particularly useful when a project has to be submitted to a client for approval before being forwarded to a commercial printer.

At the time of writing, *inCopy CS5.5* was the latest version and it permits parallel workflows; in which several people can work collaboratively on a project but in such a way that they don't stand on each others' toes. (Too many cooks in the kitchen syndrome!) In other words, an editor could work on a document without overwriting what an author is doing by way of a self-edit. It also introduced "intelligent" collaboration between editors and writers, such that an edit can either be accepted or rejected. It also supports long documents and works closely with the digital document feature of *inDesign* (see above).

QuarkXPress

As with *FrameMaker*, this software product will allow you to format pages and create a number of style sheets that you can save. These enable you to lay your text out with headers, text and captions; all appearing in a consistent manner throughout your document.

Having attended a course on using this software, I think the best way to describe *QuarkXPress* is in its role as a "closet organizer" or "closet arranger" and is similar in many respects to *Adobe inDesign*.

As a "closet organizer", you can arrange the layout of your pages and import photos, graphics, text from word processing programs, XML files and bring all of these together in one place. It gives you great control over your layout grids and is an ideal program for creating brochures, newsletters, book covers, etc. Having said that, it is also capable of handling documents of up to 2,000 pages in length or up to 2 gigabytes in size.

QuarkXPress can handle documents that range in size from 1" x 1" to 48" x 48" and can therefore be used for layouts involving everything from business cards to posters. The program can also handle multi-language documents; a feature that could be of great interest to many Canadian businesses, Federal Government and other governments together with organizations that publish bilingually in both English and French.

QuarkXPress provides you with a high level of control over text and graphics that will assist you in laying out your project. It also has many other features that are too numerous to mention and that make it a high-end desktop publishing package.

Probably one of its greatest strengths is its ability to control colours and permit colour separation for documents that you have to send for commercial printing. You can output files in PDF format. It offers you a number of Web design features which will be useful in Web authoring. *QuarkXPress 6.5* also lets you manipulate images right in the program plus it enables you to import multilayer images from *Photoshop* and manipulate them right in *Quark*.

Version 7 of *QuarkXPress* permits you to convert *inDesign* files for use in *QuarkXPress* using a module from Markzware Software called *ID2Q Xtensions*. In spite of the fact that Adobe is its competitor, *QuarkXPress 7* is tightly integrated with *Photoshop*. You can also control the transparency levels, direction and colour of shadows for boxes, lines and text. You can create PDF and PDF/X files from right within the program.

Quark Interactive Designer lets you create interactive *Flash* content as well as material for publishing on the Web from *QuarkXPress 7*.

Version 8 of *QuarkXPress* is more intuitive to use than was the case with previous versions. It has undergone a major redesign of its user interface as well as a new structure to its toolbox. One really nice feature allows you to click on a box and it will bring up the right tool set for that box. For example, if the box contains a photo, it will bring up a tool box which allows you to crop, resize and rotate the photo.

QuarkXPress is a high-end program. It's also very expensive but if you are involved professionally in publishing, it should be an indispensable part of your software library.

AdobeBridge

Adobe Bridge owes its origin to being a file browser in *Adobe Photoshop*. It is now a stand-alone software package which acts as a control centre for all of the image files from different programs contained in the *Creative Suite*.

It was first introduced in *Creative Suite 2* and has since been enhanced for users of *Creative Suites 3, 4* and *5*. In spite of this, it appears that many people have a reluctance to use *Adobe Bridge* and Adobe has been trying to overcome this reluctance.

Adobe Bridge can be used in conjunction with the following programs:

- *Adobe Photoshop*
- *Adobe Illustrator*
- *Adobe inDesign*
- *Adobe Acrobat*
- *Dreamweaver*
- *Flash*
- *Fireworks*
- *Contribute*
- *FlashPlayer.*

When you visit the "Bridge Centre" you can open up any of your recent files that you have created using any of the above programs. In addition, you can also save these files as a group, which is very useful when you have been using different programs which all relate to the same project that you're working on. Another big advantage of using *Bridge* is that you can define the colours and their settings across all programs that you are using in that group. This is a powerful tool for colour management which allows you to control the colours in any specific project.

If you are working as a team on a project, Bridge Centre makes it easy for members of the team to collaborate with one another.

When you are in the Bridge Centre, you can scroll through the files that you have saved in *Photoshop* and rank them according to their useful characteristics in your project; all of this without actually opening *Photoshop*. Another feature of Bridge Centre permits you to look at earlier versions of your work simply by using "the version cue" feature. In this way, you have access to all the earlier files that you have created so that you can always go back and select an earlier version.

Bridge supports all file formats of Adobe including those of *Adobe Acrobat*. It is not necessary to exit *Bridge* in order to take a look at an *Acrobat* file. In the preview mode you are able to view all file formats which are used in *Adobe Photoshop* and you can preview them by using the zoom tool. In this regard, a large monitor can help for viewing, since things can become very crowded on a small screen.

One of the biggest strengths of *Adobe Bridge* is the way in which it is able to handle Encapsulated Postscript (EPS) Files which are used in pre-press and in commercial printing. In order to convert files when you are in *the Adobe Bridge*, you simply drag them into the preview pane and you will see the introductory thumbnail. This is in contrast to looking at an EPS file in its native format, since it can be very hard to discern what the files about since a thumbnail can be very "pixelated" (i.e., jagged) and not clear. So, the advantage of working in *Adobe Bridge* is that you can click on the icon and get a larger image of the preview.

You can group photos or files. Thus, you can create a "Photo Stack" and drag and drop other photos onto that stack. You should note that the original files are not altered in any way when your place them into a stack.

One feature introduced in the *CS3* version is the filter panel which lets you quickly locate files. *Bridge Centre* formerly offered the user access to over a million royalty free photos, however, this service was discontinued effective April 1, 2008.

At the time of writing the latest version was *Adobe Bridge CS5*. To quote Adobe, "it is a powerful media manager that provides centralized access to all your creative assets."

Chapter 12

Some Speciality Programs that Can Help

Thompson Reuters Endnote

Endnote was initially published by Niles Software Inc. and later acquired by Thompson Reuters.

Endnote is the ultimate software if you are a researcher, academic or librarian who wants to set up bibliographies at the end of documents. This software works hand-in-glove with *WordPerfect* and *Microsoft Word*. In both these word processing programs, it can be accessed from the tools pull-down menu. It also works with the former *AmiPro* (now called *WordPro*) by Lotus, together with any documents created in Rich Text Format (RTF), which was discussed in an earlier chapter.

Endnote lets you create your own database of references and stores them in a number of libraries. Each library can contain up to 32,000 references and you can link these to full text articles on the World Wide Web. You can also open over 100 predefined connection files while you are conducting online searches. You can easily search these bibliographic databases using the *Endnote* search window. In addition, you can transfer references from the Web to your own *Endnote* library.

Endnote is a very neat add-on program if you are involved in publishing academic or research documents. *EndNote 8* provided you with unicode support for any language plus new reference types and fields. *Endnote X1*, lets you create up to 500 customized groups in each library.

A new tab has been created in *Word 2007* to replace the tools menu of earlier versions. This makes the options for "Cite While You Write" easy to locate and select with just one click.

A new file attachment field permits you to organize up to 45 files per reference.

EndNote Web is a companion product which is a Web-based reference organizer incorporated into the *ISI Web of Knowledge* that can be used by researchers to search across multiple resources simultaneously. This *ISI Web of Knowledge* boasts of 20 million users worldwide.

Researchers and others involved with technical writing will find that version, *Endnote X3*, will help them in creating bibliographies and in creating citations as they write. It is closely tied in with *ResearchID* which provides unique identifiers to scholars on a world-wide basis, thereby helping to eliminate the chances of misidentification. It also offers access to over 3,900 online sources and journal styles.

Endnote X4 introduced a new feature with its "Cite While You Write" which works with Microsoft *Word 2010*. You can also import and search PDF files.

At the time of writing, the latest version was *Thompson Reuters Endnote X5*. A new feature lets you attach files to an *EndNote* Web record and to preview and annotate any PDF files which are attached. One very powerful new feature lets you update references automatically and to compare duplicate references.

AccentExpress

Accent Express is a very serious and comprehensive program that'll be a great benefit if you are involved with writing in foreign languages. It features more than 20 languages and there is no restriction on the number of different languages that can be used in any one document. Almost all of the major European languages are there, including Greek, Russian, Polish and Czech. It also includes Hebrew and a simplified version of Arabic. It does not include Chinese, any of the Far Eastern languages or African languages.

I must say that I was very impressed with the level of sophistication shown by this program. For example, it differentiates between French as it is written in France and Québeçois. It also distinguishes between Spanish and Mexican Spanish. The same is true of Italian, French and German written in Switzerland.

When you install the program, you are prompted to choose which languages you wish to work in and the language that you want to use for your help files and other documentation. It should be noted that your help files and the menu languages are only available in 20 of the more popular languages.

A series of keyboard maps are available that will allow you to use your keyboard to import foreign characters into your document. For example, by pressing the "~" key at the top left corner of your keyboard, at the same time as pressing the numeral "7", you can create the French "e" with a grave accent: "è".

An even easier way is to click on the individual characters on a representation of a keyboard which appears on your monitor. This has been designed in such a way as to take up less than one-quarter of your screen and it can be moved by dragging it to whatever location you find convenient. Typing is easy--simply click the keys with your mouse!

The program also includes 40 *TrueType* fonts and 7 alphabet/character sets.

In addition to the *Express Version* of this software, there is a "Special Edition" and a "Professional" version available; each of which contain more fonts and spell checkers, Thesauruses and a Berlitz interpreter which will do word-for-word translations in the five languages. These software packages will be of great assistance if your business is involved in import/export or your local market is segmented into ethnic groups.

You can import or export your work from and to *WordPerfect*, *Word*, *AmiPro*, *Excel*, *Lotus 1-2-3* and in RTF and ASCII formats.

My latest search suggests that this software may be quite difficult to locate and potential users may have to settle for versions from several years ago; if indeed they can be sourced. Some "free" downloads are available on the Web but I will admit that I have not checked them out.

Chapter 13

Some Help with Creating or Importing Text

Getting Text into Your Documents

In this chapter, I will take a look at ways in which to import text into your documents either by using voice dictation or by scanning it.

Voice Dictation Software

By voice dictation, I mean quite literally talking into a microphone and having those words appear on your monitor, either in the voice dictation software window or in the window of one of the more popular word processing programs. Later, I'll take a quick look at three of the most well-known voice dictation packages.

Most of the text in this book has been entered by voice dictation using one of these popular programs. I have been using the software for several years now and find it extremely useful when I am creating long documents. I will confess that it is less useful for short letters or memos, since I can usually type these faster (even using two fingers) than the time it takes to activate the software; put on and adjust the microphone headset!

Voice dictation has moved a long way in the last six years. Thus, I remember watching several demonstrations about eight years ago in which the person who was demonstrating the program had to speak in distinct words with a pause in between each. This-- meant-- that -- you-- had-- to-- talk-- as--if--you-- were-- talking-- to-- some-- dumb-- robot-- !

This has all changed since the latest versions of these leading brands of voice dictation systems will now handle continuous speech. This means that you can talk normally; however, in practice, it still requires you to enunciate your words clearly so that they can be comprehended.

Voice dictation will not produce a perfect document, at least for most users, however, I find that I can get close to 99% accuracy if I concentrate on what I am saying and make sure that I am speaking clearly; with each word enunciated separately.

The key to successful voice dictation lies in the training of your software to be able to recognize your voice and the manner in which you speak. To help you in this regard, each of the programs requires you to go through a series of exercises by way of reading different material, so that the program can distinguish your speech patterns. It will then save these files and compare the noises that are coming out of your mouth to those which are saved in memory and.... eureka! It will come up with the text on your monitor!

I have found that with training, I could dictate at a speed close to 160 words per minute, which is light years faster than the five or six words per minute that I was used to when I was using two fingers on my computer keyboard! Having said this, there are several additional factors to be taken into consideration.

The first is that the 160 words per minute assumes that you have got all your thoughts in order, so that you can maintain that high-speed of dictation. I must confess, that when I type with two fingers, at about five or six words per minute,

I am typing at the same speed at which I think! This may sound a little facile, however, as a writer, I am attempting to concentrate on my sentence and paragraph structures so as to create something that is clear and concise when people come to read it.

You may find it very useful to have a second monitor (which is possible using *Windows 98, ME, 2000, XP, Vista* or *Windows 7*) upon which you have placed an outline of what you want to talk about--broken down into paragraph by paragraph details.

One of the challenges faced by voice recognition software is making a distinction between words that sound the same but have different spelling. Thus, the words: "two", "too" and "to" have similar pronunciation but are spelled differently. The only way in which the software can distinguish between the spellings is to take the word and compare it with the context in which it is used. For this reason, large files have to be maintained in computer memory so that the necessary comparisons can be made. In addition, processing speeds must be high in order that these comparisons can be made quickly.

These voice dictation packages are very memory-intensive and require a lot of Random Access Memory (RAM) in order to operate properly. This is because they are continually comparing your spoken words with the files for those sounds that they have retained in memory. For this reason you also need to use a fairly fast computer, i.e., a Pentium III or a Pentium IV.

As I mentioned above, you can voice dictate directly into several of the popular word processing programs. Thus, I have dictated directly into *WordPerfect* and *Microsoft Word* using *Dragon Naturally Speaking*.

I personally have found that the most effective way to use the software is to dictate one or two pages of text; go back over them and correct them while the ideas are still fresh in my mind and then copy and paste them to my word processing application.

There are several ways in which you can make corrections. The first is to stop every time you see a mistake coming up on your monitor and instruct the cursor to go back to that word or words that were incorrect and make the necessary corrections using your microphone. In practice, I have found this to be very time-consuming and it is also very distracting to my thought process when I are trying to create some literary masterpiece! I find it better to complete a couple of pages of text before stopping. Then, I make corrections using my cursor and keyboard.

Unlike performing an OCR scan on a document (we'll deal with this in more detail below), where you may get one or two individual characters in a word that are incorrect, continuous speech voice dictation is always comparing what you are saying with the information that it has on file. Therefore, when it misinterprets a word, it is quite possible that it will misinterpret everything else in that sentence and you will end up with a pile of incomprehensible mumbo jumbo! For this reason, I find that it is important to go over your work after every couple of pages in order to discover this mumbo jumbo because, if you leave it for several days (as I did initially), you may have no idea of what it was that you were talking about in the first place! (Of course you can play back the audio recording but this can be a klutzy exercise.)

Changes in your voice can alter the performance of these programs, however, I have found that even with a bad cold or flu, my voice dictation deteriorated only slightly. I can vouch for that, since I had the flu when I initially dictated this section!

Voice dictation will only get better as time goes by and as the programs capitalize on the ever increasing levels of computing power offered by Intel and AMD.

Another exciting area involves the use of digital recorders. Some of these can record several hours dictation, which can later be downloaded into your voice dictation software. This makes you independent of your computer when you want to write a report or letter. Do it in the park, on your sailboat, wherever!

It is conceivable that voice dictation will move into an entirely new realm in the foreseeable future, when documents can be simultaneously translated into a number of different foreign languages at the time they are being dictated. This has tremendous implications for the World Wide Web as it expands into other languages and cultures and away from English, which has been the predominant language since its inception.

For people who are slow typists or those who can't type at all, voice dictation software is a Godsend. Even experienced typists can increase their productivity. This is a very exciting technology and one which still has a long way to go--and it can only get better!

Dragon Naturally Speaking

"Wow!" What a fantastic program! I have used an earlier version and was very favourably impressed at that time and *Version 9* represented a very significant advance in bringing voice dictation software to the desktop by using the microphone and headset included in the software package. Alternatively, you can use a mobile recording device and upload your dictation at a later point in time.

This text is being dictated a short while after I installed the program and as you can see, it is doing a very commendable job. It allows me to dictate at a fairly high speed of up to 160 words per minute which would put most dictation secretaries out of business or at very least, heading towards nervous breakdowns!

The initial training only takes a few minutes and it is helpful if you speak very distinctly and enunciate your words clearly. You also have to make sure that the microphone is correctly positioned a short distance from your mouth and that you pause between commands. Such commands can be to create a new paragraph or to add punctuation marks, including quotations and brackets.

You can tell the microphone in this program to go to sleep, just as if you are talking to a dog! Then, you can tell it to wake up! However, it cannot be trained to bark at strangers or fetch your slippers!

In this exercise I want to see how the bold feature works. **It works just fine!** Okay, now that I am out of the bold feature, I can continue normally.

The *Dragon* toolbar can be placed in various locations on your window, however, I find that placing it at the top makes it very accessible and easy to use. In addition, you can use the "Extras" button to access additional features.

The program has voice commands which allow you to move to the end of your document; to the beginning, or to another location.

You can also play back what you have just dictated. This is a very important feature since you can review what you have just completed to make sure that it is correct. I tend to do this for every few pages of text that I have dictated so that they can be checked to make sure that the text correctly matches what I have said (before I forget!).

Alternatively, you can have the entire document read to you using the synthesised voice featured in the program. This can also be useful when you are proofreading. In my experience, I have found that it is always a challenge to proof read my own work and many errors tend to go undetected. By having the document read aloud, I find that errors are much more readily detected.

The playback command works with versions of *Microsoft Word*, starting with *Version 97* through to *2003*, as well as Corel *WordPerfect* Versions 8 and 9 and with *Lotus Notes*.

If several different people are using your computer, you can set each of them up as a new user with their own profile.

In the initial setup, you'll be asked which of five English dialects you wish to select between US English, UK English, Australian English, Indian English and South-East Asia English. For some reason Canadian English is not included! However, most Canucks can get away with using UK English....eh! Different versions of this software are also available for the medical and legal professions.

The package contains a small one-page summary sheet of common voice commands and I find this very useful for navigating through the document, inserting punctuation, formatting, selecting text and cutting and pasting, etc.

If you have difficulty with an unusual word, you can always spell it simply by saying "Spell C-a-n-u-c-k".

In practice, however, I find that having a keyboard handy can make life a lot more simple since there are always a few glitches and sometimes it's easier just to type in a word or phrase that is causing a problem. This prevents your blood pressure from getting too high and also avoids the temptation of yelling at your computer!

I also find that it is easier to dictate your entire document and then go back and make the corrections using your keyboard; in spite of the fact that I could do this using voice commands. This helps me avoid some of the frustration which in altering my text and also speeds up the entire process of voice dictation.

Dragon Naturally Speaking Professional 9 is tightly integrated with the *Microsoft Office Suite* and permits you to navigate in any of their applications. Thus, I have just dictated this section directly into *Microsoft Word 2003*. In addition, you can also work directly in *Excel*, *PowerPoint*, *Outlook* and *Internet Explorer*.

I should point out that you don't have to use an outside word processing program since it features a version of Microsoft's *WordPad* called *DragonPad*, which offers all the basic word processing tools and formatting but is specifically optimized for dictation. The documents created in *DragonPad* can be moved via the clipboard to other programs such as *WordPerfect*, *Word*, etc. I use *DragonPad* quite extensively and find that I can operate in a reduced-size window while I am operating some other program. Also, it takes up less memory which can be helpful if you are operating a number of programs simultaneously. But, before purchasing this program, you should make sure that you can meet the minimum system requirements, which are as follows:

1) Intel Pentium 4 or higher
2) 512 MB Ram
3) one GB of free disk space

4)   Microsoft *Windows XP* or higher
5)   a 16-bit soundcard
6)   CD-ROM drive for installation
7)   speakers for playback
8)   a noise-cancelling headset (included in the package)
9)   a Web connection for activation.

In summary, this is an excellent program and I'm very impressed with the way it has developed into a very powerful tool which you can use and save yourself a lot of time and money; especially if your typing speed is very slow, like mine!

Unfortunately, I have not had the opportunity to review Version 10 but supposedly it is 20% more accurate than Version 9 and now permits you to format your work with a single command. It also works on the 64 bit versions of *Vista* and *Windows 7*. The minimum requirements are the same as for Version 9.

At the time of writing, the latest version was *11.5*. This boasts of improved accuracy and easier methods to make corrections, to apply formatting and make editing changes. As with previous versions, it will work in conjunction with a digital recorder, so you don't have to lug your PC or your laptop with you. In addition, you can now post your dictation directly to Twitter and Facebook, if you are into using social media.

L&H VoiceXpress

L&H VoiceXpress Professional, is targeted towards business professionals who use *Microsoft Office*; in particular *Word, Excel, PowerPoint, Outlook* and *Windows Explorer*. With these programs you can employ a number of intuitive commands using "Natural Language Technology". As mentioned above, this allows you to voice activate editing and formatting commands in these programs, in addition to performing dictation. This program comes with four specialized plug-in voeabularies covering:

- business and finance
- leisure
- technology
- in the news.

This program has a "Talk and Go" feature in which it will accept dictation from a number of hand-held digital dictation devices. This is an excellent feature if you are on the road a lot.

L&H VoiceXpress comes with a "QuickTour" which leads you through the basics. A series of "QuickStart" exercises demonstrate how to perform specific tasks. An "Audio Setup Wizard" helps you to configure the microphone and tune it. In addition, you are recommended to train the program using "Speaker Enrollment". This usually takes about one to two hours. You can perform ongoing training and correction by means of the "Voice Xpress" correction window.

This program has a 22,000 to 30,000 vocabulary of words which it recognizes. In addition, a "Vocabulary Extender" enables you to add your own words to the program's vocabulary. Words which you would probably want to include are those specific to your business or industry. You might also want to include acronyms.

L&H VoiceXpress can also read documents back to you through the use of its "Text to Speech" engine. The program package also includes a high quality microphone headset.

The latest version that I am aware of is *Version 5* but it does not appear to have been updated since 2000.

ViaVoice

ViaVoice by IBM is another leading brand of voice-recognition software which also works with the Natural Language Commands contained in *Microsoft Word*. It is now supported by ScanSoft Inc. It will work on *Windows*, Macintosh and handheld platforms. As with the previous two products, *ViaVoice* lets you dictate in continuous speech.

This program contains a 64,000 word basic vocabulary of recognizable words and a further 250,000 word back-up dictionary. If the word which the program detects is not in either of these, you can add it to your personal vocabulary, which has the capacity to add a further 64,000 words.

ViaVoice also lets you activate a number of "mini-vocabularies" while you dictate. These cover the topics: business, computers and cuisine.

The program contains a set-up for your microphone and some basic training. Like the previous voice dictation systems which I reviewed, *ViaVoice* offers training to improve recognition accuracy.

An enrollment option enables you to enroll more than once. This would cover situations where the ambient background noise is different (such as on an aeroplane) or when you are using a recording device in conjunction with *ViaVoice*. This feature also covers the use of different microphones.

As with the two voice dictation programs which I reviewed above, *ViaVoice* also allows you to play back your dictation through your computer speakers. This "ViaVoice Outloud" feature enables you to hear what you said and correct what you wrote.

The most recent and advanced edition is *Version 10* which includes a noise-cancelling headset/microphone and support for digital handheld recorders. It also has a "Command and Control" system of voice navigation macros that will work when surfing the Web as well as many popular *Windows* applications.

More recently, IBM had added *Embedded ViaVoice* speech technology to mobile devices and automobile components.

Optical Character Recognition (OCR) Software

I will now show you another way in which text can be inputted into your documents by scanning them and using an Optical Character Recognition or "OCR" program.

The text must first be scanned using a scanner. Alternatively, it could be received as a fax and brought into your fax software program as an electronic file. In both these cases, the quality of the original document is of vital importance for the OCR software to work properly and provide you with a satisfactory result. Most OCR software can read different styles of fonts with a reasonable degree of accuracy, however, I have found that text which is created in the Helvetica or Arial fonts produces the best results. At the other end of the spectrum, script and fancy fonts will give you a lot of trouble.

In the case where poor quality photocopies are used either for scanning or faxing, the OCR software may have a hard time making sense of the document, with the result that your output will be garbled to the point that it may be useless.

A good, clean original presented for OCR can produce a 98% or better accuracy. So, it is well worth the time to make sure that the original is of the highest quality possible.

One feature which can be used to improve the quality of a faxed document is a document cleanup facility, which was available on some fax programs such as earlier versions of *WinFax*. By employing this feature, you can cleanup the document of many little specs and spots, which would otherwise cause a problem with the optical character recognition.

There are several brands of OCR software available on the market, but I will only examine one in this chapter.

OmniPage Professional

OmniPage Professional is a very highly regarded OCR program published by Nuance. It will operate under most *Windows* operating systems commencing with the second edition of *Windows 98*, *Windows ME*, *Windows 2000*, *Windows XP* and *Windows Server 2003*. However, it will only operate with certain scanners and you are advised to check the compatibility of your scanner with those listed as being suitable on the Nuance Web site.

This version of *OmniPage* has a 25% better accuracy than the previous version, according to the publisher. It does this using new tools to improve scan quality, which in turn, improves the optical character recognition process. Another of its new features is a "character map" which makes it possible to handle certain character images such as trademark symbols or copyright marks.

If you've ever tried scanning text on coloured paper, you will know that the OCR process does not always work very well, however, in this version of *OmniPage* the text will stand out much more clearly, allowing for a much more accurate OCR to take place.

Dictionaries have been built into many languages and these can be supplemented by the user who can add words; edit them or remove them. In addition, there is a "Verifer Tool" which lets you compare the completed OCR document with the original scanned document.

This program allows you to edit graphics if you have an image editor installed on your computer. It also has a "Text Editor" which displays tables as grids and allows you to modify the table and move gridlines. This has always been a major challenge for OCR software. It can also handle text contained in frames by using a special "Shortcut Menu".

For users who are visually impaired, there is a "ScanSoft RealSpeak" feature which will read an OCR document out aloud. This can also be useful for anybody checking the accuracy of a scanned document that has undergone OCR.

One outstanding feature of this program is its ability to work with forms either in paper or electronic format. Thus, the program is capable of producing a blank form which can be saved in a PDF, RTF or other format. The blank areas of such forms can then be filled in. This is definitely a boon for business people who are bogged down with government bureaucracy; municipal bureaucracy; meeting employment standards; filling out tax forms; applying for credit; responding to surveys together with a maddening host of other paperwork involving forms.

Another very powerful feature is the option to select a formatting level.

Plain text: which features left-aligned text in a single font and font size.

Formatted text: which accommodates different size fonts and paragraph styling together with graphics and tables.

Flowing page: which retains the original layout of the page including columns but not text boxes or frames.

Text page: which keeps the original layout of the page with text, pictures and tables.

Spreadsheet: which recognizes a table and places results in a tabular format and is especially useful for saving tables that occupy a full-page.

Finally, files can be saved in various PDF formats; with or without images, or even as image only files. Files can also be saved in an audio wave file and these can later be listened to in ScanSoft's *RealSpeak*. In addition, files can be exported to a central server or to Microsoft's *SharePoint*.

All in all, this program is the leading application if you want to use OCR to scan your documents and bring them into a word processing program, a spreadsheet or to have them converted into a PDF. It will also assume greater importance if Microsoft's *SharePoint* gains in popularity.

Version 16 boasted a 27% increase in document conversion accuracy compared to the previous release. Nuance also claims that it works 46% faster and the program now comes bundled with *PaperPort 11 Professional* (see below).

One interesting new development is that you can now use OCR on images from your digital camera e.g., it could scan the message on a sign and some new technology lets it adjust for any 3-D perspectives.

Another big advance in the new version is the ability to turn paper forms into editable PDF forms. Not only that, it can now extract the data from either PDF or printed forms and place it into a spreadsheet or database.

OmniPage Version 17, boasts of improved accuracy for scanned documents as well as for those in PDF and digital formats. It is tightly integrated with *Microsoft Office* and features a one-click toolbar so you can convert your documents quickly. The processing speed is now 21% faster if you are operating on a quad-core computer. It can scan documents in over 120 different languages. It offers support for i-phone and 2 megapixel phone cameras.

At the time of writing, the latest version was *OmniPage Professional 18*. Once more the accuracy has been further improved and it can now handle tables, columns and bulleted items. It can convert a document into readable text for upload to an Amazon Kindle eBook reader.

Chapter 14

Document Management

Nuance PaperPort

Nuance PaperPort is a leader in document management for the PC. It comprises three separate entities and I will cover each of these individually.

Firstly, it will work with documents that you have scanned and allows you to enhance them and manipulate them. For example, you can straighten the document that has been scanned at an angle and this is one feature which I greatly appreciate, since most scanning software is not able to handle such an adjustment. You can also crop documents and rotate them.

You can import photographs from a digital camera and again the program offers some rudimentary editing capabilities.

The "Capture Assistant" allows you to assemble the pages in your current scan and add additional pages if you need before it is saved to the *PaperPort* desktop. This Capture Assistant lets you review pages as they are scanned. You can also rotate pages, insert blank ones and even place pages in a different order from the one in which they were scanned.

You can also use a tool in this program to improve the quality of the scans, either on a page-by-page basis, or for the entire assembled document.

You can use the OCR feature to convert scanned documents into text.

Secondly, the program operates as a document management system with a specialized desktop which has been designed to handle documents; especially those that have been scanned. Thus, you could take a scanned document and conduct OCR and then drag it over to a *Microsoft Word* icon situated at the bottom of your screen and it will automatically be converted into a *Word* document. Equally, you could take the same scanned document and drag it on top of an *Adobe Reader* icon and it will be converted into a PDF file.

Nuance has designed its own software for creating PDF files and this is referred to as "Create 3"which uses a file compression system known as "PDF-MCR". This will generate files which are about 1/8 of the size of regular PDF files. Obviously, this is an important feature when it comes to archiving business paperwork on a computer, or a server, or external backup storage device.

One interesting feature of the software is that it enables you to stack a group of PDF files into a single PDF. You can also overlay one PDF over another.

It also lets you combine files from different applications into one PDF document. For example, you could combine files from *Microsoft Word* or *Excel* and *PowerPoint* into one PDF document.

You can also stack a number of *PaperPort* images into a single file and the program allows you to un-stack them at a later stage.

One very powerful feature of this program lets you search through PDF files to find a specific item. Thus, you can open a "Search Pane" which permits you to search all of the files in a specific folder or subfolder, or even all of your *PaperPort* folders. This is a very powerful feature if you want to search through archived material to find something specific that you need.

The program also lets you add notes and annotations to your files; to highlight certain areas on the page or type in text with a transparent background. You can also draw with a pencil in freehand or you could place a stamp mark on a page e.g., "confidential".

Probably one of the most exciting aspects of this program is its ability to let you fill out forms. As any business person knows, there is nothing more irritating than spending hours filling out forms by hand, especially if the quality of your handwriting leaves a lot to be desired; like mine!

The way this works is that you would scan in a blank form and drag the scanned form on to the "Form Typer" icon in the "Send to Bar".

Alternatively, you would take a form that has been delivered by e-mail as an attachment in *Microsoft Word* format or as a PDF form. This would then be dragged onto the Form Typer icon.

Once you are in Form Typer, you can fill out the form by stepping through the fields until it is completed and then generate the output as a PDF which can then be forwarded.

The third component in this software package is *PaperPort Watson* which is a Web, e-mail and document search assistant.

It is an intelligent search utility program which unites the best features of popular search engines such as *Google*, *Yahoo!* and *MSN* together with any desktop search utilities that has been installed on your PC. This will bring together information from the Web, e-mail, news sites, blogs and shopping sites and display them on a sidebar on your desktop where you can click on them to bring up the full Web page or story.

This program should not be confused with *Dr. Watson*, which is a Microsoft utility which is used to detect and decode errors which occur when a *Windows* program is running or in *Windows* itself. It is unfortunate that the same name has been used because they are completely different utilities which serve totally different purposes.

In order to conduct a search using *PaperPort Watson*, you would simply enter your query in the search box and then click on the little green button bar. It will combine the search results and display them on the sidebar under the subheadings of Web, news, blogs, shopping and desktop. It will also give a total of all the search results at the top of the bar.

I've tried this product out, however, I have found that the number of search results can be quite modest compared to the same search conducted on *Google*. Thus, a search for my name on *Watson* came up with 67 search results compared to over half a million on *Google*! Obviously, *Google* listed many other people with similar names. One big advantage however, is that it did include news items and also specifically delegated certain items to the shopping category; relating to some of the books which I have written.

Version 12 featured faster display of PDF files, together with a "scan now" button which no longer requires you to go to the scanner settings view. There are many other new features and improvements but one which really appeals to me is the search capabilities for scanned documents. Thus, you can use a search engine such as *Google* or *Windows Desktop Search* to find keywords, phrases or files on your PC or on your network.

At the time of writing, the latest was *Version 14*. This lets you work with cloud based documents plus you can work from any location. You can now create new notes or add notes to an existing document. It also features improved scanning of documents.

This is powerful stuff!

Chapter 15

When Gutenberg Turned in His Grave

From the Gutenberg Printing Press to eBooks

It was 1450 when a German blacksmith, named Johannes Gensfleisch zur Laden zum Gutenberg, created the first printing press and made the work of many monks and scribes completely unnecessary.

Jump ahead to 1971, when the first digital books or eBooks made their appearance and the first digital library was created. It was named appropriately enough, as Project Gutenberg, in honour of the world's first print-on-paper book printer. According to Marie Lebert of the University of Toronto, the initial concept was to allow people to own their own digital library made up of copyright free books. The project received a tremendous boost with the development of the World Wide Web in 1990 and is still with us today.

In the meanwhile, many publishers and book sellers have entered the fray and are offering eBooks as well as print-on-paper books for sale on a commercial basis. Initial adoption was slow but as more and more eBook readers, tablets and intelligent phones flooded the market, eBooks have come of age. Indeed, a study by Barclay's Capital suggested that a quarter of all book sales by 2015 will be made up of eBooks. Obviously, every publisher has to pay close attention in order to survive.

If you want to know more about publishing your work as an eBook, I would recommend another book published in 2012 by Productive Publications of Toronto: *eBook Publishing for Beginners: How to Make Money Selling Your Digital Books Online* by www.Learn2succeed.com. It will take you onto the next step in the exciting new world of digital publishing and yes: it's available in eBook format as well as in softcover!

Desktop Publishing Covers a Wide Spectrum

As you can see from what I have written, the words "desktop publishing" cover a wide variety of activities. Some of you may be looking to preparing books or reports; whereas others may simply be interested in creating a simple brochure, a greeting card or a business card. Hopefully, this short guide will have provided you with some appreciation for what is available from software vendors. In other words, I hope I have provided a springboard from which you can leap into more detail.

Thank you for accompanying me on this review.

Good Luck with your publishing projects!

PRODUCTIVE PUBLICATIONS

Our 27th Year Publishing Non-Fiction Books
to Help You Meet the Challenges of the Digital Age

Other Great Books to Help You Check Them Out!

You will find brief outlines in the following pages but for more details and chapter contents, visit our Web sites as follows:

USA and Overseas: *www.ProductivePublications.com*
Canada: *www.ProductivePublications.ca*

You can order using a credit card as follows:

Order Desk USA and Canada Phone Toll-Free: 1-(877) 879-2669
Fax Order Form on the last page to: (416) 322-7434
Enquiries Phone: (416) 483-0634
Place Secure Orders Online at:

USA and Overseas: *www.ProductivePublications.com*
Canada: *www.ProductivePublications.ca*

E-mail orders to: *ProductivePublications@rogers.com*

Snail Mail Orders to: Productive Publications
P. O. Box 7200, Station A
Toronto, ON M5W 1X8 Canada

Courier Orders to: Productive Publications
7-B Pleasant Blvd., #1210
Toronto, ON M4T 1K2 Canada

**eBook Publishing
for Beginners**

**How to Make Money
Selling Your Digital
Books Online**

**By: Learn2succeed.com
Incorporated**

Barclay's Capital has suggested that a quarter of all worldwide book sales in 2015 will be made up of eBooks. This is wake-up call to publishers who are still trapped in the print-on-paper world. It also has ramifications for bookstores, libraries and the book supply chain .

112 pages; Softcover; ISBN: 978-1-55270-456-1   CIP
Canada: $19.99 US: $19.99 UK: $12.59

**Desktop Publishing
for Beginners**

**How to Create Great
Looking Brochures,
Books and Documents**

**By: Learn2succeed.com
Incorporated**

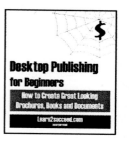

This book will introduce you to desktop publishing and shows you how you can create your own brochures, books and documents. It is s, although some are available for the Macintosh.

114 pages; Softcover; ISBN: 978-1-55270-455-4   CIP
Canada: $19.99 US: $19.99 UK: $12.59

**Gold Investing
for Beginners**

**An Opportunity for Huge
Gains or a Bubble About
to Burst?**

**By: Learn2succeed.com
Incorporated**

Find out about the major factors which influence the price of gold and determine for yourself whether a gold bubble has developed and is about to burst or whether investing in gold still offers an opportunity to make huge gains.

134 page; Softcover, ISBN: 978-1-55270-445 CIP
Canada $19.99 US: $19.99 UK: $12.59

**Stock Market Investing
for Beginners**

**How to Increase Your
Wealth in Uncertain Times**

**By: Learn2succeed.com
Incorporated**

Written for people who are fed up with the paltry interest their bank pays on their savings accounts as well as those who are sadly disillusioned with the lackluster performance of their investment advisors. Everything you need to know to get started.

164 pages, Softcover; ISBN: 978-1-55270-446-2   CIP
Canada: $24.95 US: $24.95 UK: $15.79

**For details visit our Canadian Web site: *www.ProductivePublications.ca*
American Web site: *www.ProductivePublications.com*
Order securely online or mail the order form at the end of this catalogue
Phone our Order Desk toll-free at: 1-(877) 879-2669**

Digital Photography for Beginners

How to Create Great Photos for Fun or Profit

By: Learn2succeed.com Incorporated

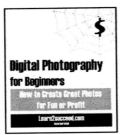

If you want to become a digital shutterbug, the place to start is by reading this excellent introduction which tries to explain everything in plain, non-technical terms.

98 pages; Softcover; ISBN: 978-1-55270-447-9   CIP
Canada $17.99 US: $1799   UK: $11.39

Time Management for Beginners

How to Get the Most Out of Every Day

By: Learn2succeed.com Incorporated

There is a saying that some people count time, while others make time count. This book is about making time count. It's about managing your time effectively so that you can get the most out of each and every day of your life.

114 pages; Softcover, ISBN: 978-1-55270-453-0   CIP
Canada: $19.99 US: $19.99 UK: $12.59

Steps to Choosing the Right Computer for Your Home or Business

A No-Nonsense Guide Which Cuts Through All the Hype

By: Learn2succeed.com Incorporated

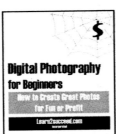

Read this book **before** you purchase a new computer. It leads you through all factors you should consider. Computer store sales people are more interested in making a commission than on selling you what you need. This book will help. Softcover;

96 pages; Softcover, ISBN: 978-1-55270-454-7   CIP
Canada: $17.99 US: $1799   UK: $11.39

Food Poisoning and Waterborne Illness

How to Prevent 1.8 Million Deaths Every Year

By: Learn2succeed.com Incorporated

Figures from the World Health Organization and the Government of Ghana, suggest that between 1.8 million and 2.2 million deaths occur every year due to food poisoning and waterborne illness. There are many ways to significantly reduce the death rate. You will find out why governments are reluctant to regulate or take steps to meet the challenge.

116 pages, Softcover; ISBN 978-1-55270-449-3   CIP
Canada: $19.99 US: $19.99 UK: $12.59

For details visit our Canadian Web site: *www.ProductivePublications.ca*
American Web site: *www.ProductivePublications.com*
Order securely online or mail the order form at the end of this catalogue
Phone our Order Desk toll-free at: 1-(877) 879-2669

Business Start-Up for Beginners

How to Become Your Own Boss

By: Learn2succeed.com Incorporated

If you have ever dreamed of starting your own business and becoming your own boss, you've taken the first important step by selecting this book. It will show you what it takes to become an entrepreneur and how to find ideas to start your own business. You will have to acquire a lot of skills very quickly and this book will alert you to some of the things you will need to know and provide you with a lot of insight, based on first-hand experience.

116 pages, Softcover; ISBN 978-1-55270-444-8;   CIP
Canada: $19.99 US: $19.99 UK: $12.59

Bank Financing for Beginners

How to Borrow Money to Grow Your Business

By: Learn2succeed.com Incorporated

This book should definitely be on your reading list before you go charging into you bank in search of a business loan. Credit conditions may be tight, but this book should increase your chances of securing a bank loan.

114 pages; Softcover; ISBN: 978-1-55270-459-2   CIP
Canada: $19.99 US: $19.99 UK: $12.59

Venture Capital Financing for Beginners

How to Raise Equity Capital from Venture Capitalists and Angels

By: Learn2succeed.com Incorporated

If you are already in business or about to start a business, this book will help you raise equity capital from traditional venture capitalists or from "angels".

110 pages; Softcover, ISBN: 978-1-55270-458-5 CIP
Canada: $19.99 US: $19.99 UK: $12.59

Public Speaking for Beginners

How to Communicate Effectively in the Digital Age

By: Learn2succeed.com Incorporated

The King's Speech, drew attention to public speaking by someone with a disability. Even if you don't have a disorder, speaking in public can still be a challenge. This book will help you communicate effectively with your audience.

78 pages; Softcover; ISBN: 978-1-55270-452-3   CIP
Canada: $15.99 US: $15.99 UK: £9.99

For details visit our Canadian Web site: *www.ProductivePublications.ca*
American Web site: *www.ProductivePublications.com*
Order securely online or mail the order form at the end of this catalogue
Phone our Order Desk toll-free at: 1-(877) 879-2669

Your Guide to Raising Venture Capital for Your Own Business in Canada

Revised and Updated 2012-2013 Edition

By: Iain Williamson

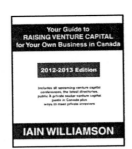

This book is a gold mine of information for anyone who is raising venture capital in Canada. It shows you how to do it yourself. It discusses the structure of the industry; what venture capitalists are looking for and how they evaluate deals. It tells you how to contact them. Find out what informal investors or "angels" can offer and how to find them. You can see if corporate angels and intermediaries can be of assistance.

232 pages, softcover; ISBN 978-1-55270-505-6 CIP
ISSN 1191-0534   Canada: $74.95

Your Guide to Arranging Bank & Debt Financing for Your Own Business in Canada

Revised and Updated 2012-2013 Edition

By: Iain Williamson

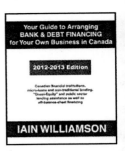

Learn the secrets of successful debt financing in Canada. Find out who the players are in Canadian banking. Do you qualify for high risk, unsecured loans? How to prepare your company before you approach lenders. Find out how your loan application is evaluated. Can factoring or leasing help you? The author has many years of experience in bank financing and leasing.

326 pages, softcover; ISBN 978-1-55270-506-3 CIP
ISSN 1191-0542 Canada: $81.95

Your Guide to Financing Business Growth by Selling a Piece of the Pie

What's involved in going public; employee share ownership plans and franchising in Canada

Revised and Updated 2012-2013 Edition

By: Iain Williamson

A critical examination of three methods of growing your business by using other peoples' money. How to sell shares to the public or to your employees. Covers the Canadian stock exchanges and their listing requirements. Includes sections on London's Alternative Investing Market (AIM) and on NASDAQ in the US. What's involved in establishing an Employee Share Ownership Plan (ESOP). How to expand through franchising. The author was a financial analyst in the Canadian stockbrokerage business for five years.

140 pages, softcover; ISBN 978-1-55270-507-0 CIP
ISSN 1191-0488: Canada: $46.95

Your Guide to Canadian Export Financing: Successful Techniques for Financing Your Exports from Canada

Revised 2012-2013 Edition

By: Iain Williamson

Practical techniques for financing exports. Get details of all provincial and federal assistance programs that help you export including addresses and phone numbers to steer you in the right direction. Includes a chapter on insurance. The author is a consultant and entrepreneur who knows the practical side of importing and exporting. He is an entrepreneur, business consultant and seminar leader wth considerable experience in importing and exporting.

256 pages, softcover; ISBN 978-1-55270-411-0 CIP
ISSN: 1191-047X Canada: $58.95

For details visit our Canadian Web site: *www.ProductivePublications.ca*
American Web site: *www.ProductivePublications.com*
Order securely online or mail the order form at the end of this catalogue
Phone our Order Desk toll-free at: 1-(877) 879-2669

Page 4

Your Guide to Starting & Self-Financing Your Own Business in Canada

Revised 2012-2013 Edition

By: Iain Williamson

This 2012-2013 Edition has been updated and revised to reflect the many changes that have taken place in the sources of marketing information and finding it on the Internet. Shows you how to operate a business out of your home. How to use computers and the Web to run your business more efficiently. Covers computer software, building a Web site, e-commerce and selling on eBay. Helps you determine how much money you really need and whether you can self-finance your own business.

342 pages, softcover; ISBN 978-1-55270-503-2 CIP
ISSN 1191-0518 Canada: $56.95

Your Guide to Preparing a Plan to Raise Money for Your Own Business

Revised 2012-2013 Edition

By: Iain Williamson

A good business plan is essential to succeed in your quest for financing. Contains a step-by-step guide to create your own winning plan. Computer software you can use. Find out how spreadsheets can help you. Learn how to address the concerns of investors or lenders. Tips on structuring your plan. Contains a sample plan as an example. Computer software to help you make great presentations to investors or lenders.

208 pages, softcover, ISBN 978-1-55270-504-9 CIP
ISSN 1191-0496 Canada: $46.95

Your Guide to Government Financial Assistance for Business

(Separate Editions-one for each Province & Territory)

Revised 2012-2013 Editions

By: Iain Williamson

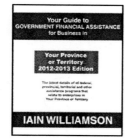

Business financing in Canada is in a constant state of flux. New government programs are continually being introduced. Old ones are often amended or discontinued with little publicity. These books will provide you with the latest information on all Federal and Provincial/Territorial programs that specifically relate to each area. Author, Iain Williamson, of Entrepreneurial Business Consultants of Canada, has over 30 years experience as a stock market financial analyst and as owner-manager of his own companies.

$89.95 ea. Softcover; CIP. Title & ISBN See list on right ➜

Your Guide to Government Financial Assistance for Business In...

EDITION	ISBN	PAGES
Newfoundland & Labrador	9781552705094	298
Prince Edward Island	9781552705100	278
Nova Scotia	9781552705117	294
New Brunswick	9781552705124	280
Quebec	9781552705131	306
Ontario	9781552705148	374
Manitoba	9781552705155	326
Saskatchewan	9781552705162	326
Alberta	9781552705179	320
British Columbia	9781552705186	306
The Yukon	9781552705193	256
The Northwest Territories	9781552705209	252
The Nunavut	9781552705216	252

Please specify Province or Territory when ordering. All titles are $89.95 each.

For details visit our Canadian Web site: *www.ProductivePublications.ca*
American Web site: *www.ProductivePublications.com*
Order securely online or mail the order form at the end of this catalogue
Phone our Order Desk toll-free at: 1-(877) 879-2669

Steps to Opening a Successful Web Store

The Basics of How to Set-Up Shop in Cyberspace

By: Learn2succeed.com Incorporated

How to find products to sell, research the market and open your own e-commerce Web site. Use online and offline advertising to drive traffic. Consider selling at eBay auctions at your own eBay store. Review the advantages of running your business from home and how to set it up. Learn how to select the best computer hardware and software. Establish your marketing strategy, prepare your marketing plan and incorporate it into your business plan. Calculate how much will it cost to start.

154 pages, softcover; ISBN 978-1-55270-357-1   CIP
Canada: $24.95 US: $24.95 UK: £15.79

Steps to Starting a Successful Retail Business

How to Find a Niche and Turn it Into a Money Machine

By: Learn2succeed.com Incorporated

Where to get ideas and direct import your own merchandise. How to research your market. Covers legal structures and tax permits. The importance of location and the hazards of lease renewals. Your store layout, fixturing, signage, lighting and window displays. Hire staff and reduce shoplifting. Use planogramming to fine-tune your operation. How to advertise and use direct marketing to augment your sales. Use e-commerce on the Web to extend your reach.

144 pages, softcover; ISBN 978-1-55270-359-5   CIP
Canada: $24.95 US: $24.95 UK: £15.79

Steps to Starting a Successful Import Business

How to Find Products, Bring Them into the Country and Make Money Selling Them

By: Learn2succeed.com Incorporated

Provides the basic knowledge you need to set up and start your own importing business and how to make money selling the products you import. How to find products to import and then do the research to find out whether you can sell them in your local market. How to pay for imports plus freight alternatives for importing your goods and what's involved with customs clearance. Look at some of the advantages of warehousing and bonded warehousing. How to use advertising, direct marketing and e-commerce to sell your imports.

148 pages, softcover, ISBN 978-1-55270-358-8   CIP
Canada: $24.95 US: $24.95 UK: £15.79

Direct Marketing for Beginners

How to Cut Out the Middleman and Sell Direct to Consumers

By: Learn2succeed.com Incorporated

Cut out the middleman and increase your profit margins. Review different methods of direct marketing and learn how to create your own Web site, attract visitors and conduct e-commerce. Take a look at permission-based e-mail and e-newsletters. Learn how to sell at auctions on eBay and set up your own eBay store. How to prepare your marketing plan. Review the laws and regulations which govern advertising and marketing together with the do-no-call lists.

160 pages, softcover; ISBN 978-1-55270-352-6   CIP
Canada: $24.95 US: $24.95 UK: £15.79

For details visit our Canadian Web site: *www.ProductivePublications.ca*
American Web site: *www.ProductivePublications.com*
Order securely online or mail the order form at the end of this catalogue
Phone our Order Desk toll-free at: 1-(877) 879-2669

Home-Based Business for Beginners

How to Start a Business on a Shoestring from Your Own Home

By: Learn2succeed.com Incorporated

If you want to run your own business out of your home, this book will provide you with all the information you need to get started. Learn about the tax and other advantages of running a home-based business. But also be alerted to some of the disadvantages including finding good employees and your legal liabilities. You will learn where to find products or services to sell and how to develop your own products. Then get help in finding out if there is a market for what you have to offer.

156 pages, softcover; ISBN 978-1-55270-353-3   CIP
Canada: $24.95 US: $24.95 UK: £15.79

Part-Time Business for Beginners

Successful Ways to Augment Your Income While Working for Someone Else

By: Learn2succeed.com Incorporated

When you are working for someone else, you probably don't want them to know you have set up your own business, so you will be given some tips on how to keep it secret. How to develop a business idea and figure out if there is a market for the product or service you have selected. Learn how to advertise and sell it. Create your own Web site and open your own Web store. Sell merchandise at eBay auctions or by opening your own eBay store. Learn about legal structures for your part-time business and government sales tax permits.

152 pages, softcover; ISBN 978-1-55270-354-0   CIP
Canada: $24.95 US: $24.95 UK: £15.79

Business Financing for Beginners

Where to Find Money to Grow Your Business

By: Learn2succeed.com Incorporated

Find out how much money you really need. How to finance during different stages of business growth; all the way from relatives and friends,to informal investors or angels. What the venture capitalists can offer and hints on negotiating with them including the due diligence process, term sheets and the legal agreement. Types of loans and how to prepare before you apply. Take a look at factoring, leasing and how to sell shares through an Initial Public Offering (IPO). What's involved in Employee Share Ownership Plans (ESOPs).

146 pages, softcover, ISBN 978-1-55270-355-7   CIP
Canada: $24.95 US: $24.95 UK: £15.79

Seven Basic Steps to Start-Up Business Success

Find a Need, Conduct Research Prepare Your Plan, Locate Financing, Start Operations, Advertise and Monitor Your Progress

By: Learn2succeed.com Inc.

Find out what people want and where to get great ideas. How to conduct market research and prepare a business plan. Decide between debt or equity. Where to find informal investors or how to get bank financing. Consider the legal form of your business, registration for sales taxes and how to protect your trademarks. Take a look at different marketinga and advertising techniques. How to use permission-based e-mail and e-newsletters. Review your progress and be prepared to change your strategy.

158 pages, softcover, ISBN 978-1-55270-360-1   CIP
Canada: $24.95 US: $24.95 UK: £15.79

For details visit our Canadian Web site: *www.ProductivePublications.ca*
American Web site: *www.ProductivePublications.com*
Order securely online or mail the order form at the end of this catalogue
Phone our Order Desk toll-free at: 1-(877) 879-2669

Streaming Video and Audio for Business

New Ways to Communicate with Your Customers, Employees and Shareholders Over the Internet

By: Learn2succeed.com Incorporated

This timely book looks at new ways for businesses to communicate over the Internet using video and audio. It includes advice on the equipment and software required, together with tips on content creation.

140 pages, softcover; ISBN 978-1-55270-302-1 CIP
Canada: $24.95 US: $24.95 UK: £15.79

Corporate Video Production on a Shoestring

Improve Your Communications with Your Customers, Employees and Shareholders

By: Learn2succeed.com Incorporated

Inexpensive digital camcorders offer great opportunities to improve communications with customers, employees and shareholders. This book covers the equipment and software required together with tips on post-production editing and hints on creating great content.

116 pages, softcover; ISBN 978-1-55270-303-8 CIP
Canada: $24.95 US: $24.95 UK: £15.79

e-Business for Beginners

How to Build a Web Site that Brings in the Dough

By: Learn2succeed.com Incorporated

Written for both new and existing businesses, this book introduces you to business on the Internet. It shows you how to create your own Web site, conduct e-commerce, attract customers and get paid. Reviews Web authoring and e-commerce software. How to make your Web site user-friendly and perform search engine optimization.

184 pages, softcover; ISBN 978-1-55270-280-2 CIP
Canada: $29.95 US: $29.95 UK: £18.99

Web Marketing for Small & Home-Based Businesses:

How to Advertise and Sell Your Products Online

By: Learn2succeed.com Incorporated

This book shows you how to advertise and sell your products or services on the Web. Learn the basics of e-commerce and some of the challenges facing online merchants. Find out about search engines and how to improve your listings with them. Keep you name in front of your customers with permission-based e-mail and electronic newsletters. Don't forget the importance of referrals. How to use traditional marketing to drive traffic to your site. Find out about the importance of web links and associate programs.

132 pages, softcover; ISBN 978-1-55270-119-5 CIP
Canada: $24.95 US: $24.95 UK: £15.79

For details visit our Canadian Web site: *www.ProductivePublications.ca*
American Web site: *www.ProductivePublications.com*
Order securely online or mail the order form at the end of this catalogue
Phone our Order Desk toll-free at: 1-(877) 879-2669

**Business Planning
for Beginners**

**Find Out How Much Money
You Will Need to
Run Your Business**

By: Learn2succeed.com
Incorporated

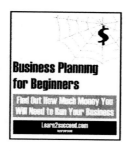

Covers your operational, marketing and advertising plans. Examines the impact of the Internet. Covers human resource requirements and sub-contracting, automation or computerization to minimize staffing requirements. Set strategic objectives and calculate how much money you will need. Covers the manufacturing, service, retail and construction businesses. Printing your plan. How to use it as a financing document and make effective presentations to potential investors or lenders.

150 pages, softcover, ISBN 978-1-55270-356-4 CIP
Canada: $24.95 US: $24.95 UK: £15.79

**Advertising for
Beginners**

**Successful Web and
Online Advertising
in the Digital Age**

By: Learn2succeed.com
Incorporated

This book emphasises less expensive forms of advertising such as direct mail, print media, yellow pages, signage, trade shows, telemarketing and fax broadcasting. Less emphasis is placed on broadcast media, since this tends to be expensive and often beyond the budget of smaller companies. It shows you how to establish an effective Web presence and how to use offline media to drive traffic to your Web site. Learn how to prepare your advertising plan and the standards and laws which apply to advertising and privacy.

146 pages, softcover; ISBN 978-1-55270-351-9 CIP
Canada: $24.95 US: $24.95 UK: £15.79

**Steps to Starting a
Recession-Proof Business**

**Where to Find Ideas and
How to Start**

By: Learn2succeed.com
Incorporated

Recessions are tough times to start a business and it is imperative to choose one that will survive. This book provides a lot of tips on finding areas which will survive and prosper during a severe economic downturn. It also shows readers how to set up their business and keep their start-up costs to a minimum.

141 pages, softcover; ISBN 978-1-55270-381-6 CIP
Canada: $24.95 US: $24.95 UK: £15.79

**Self-Employment
for Beginners**

**How to Create Your Own
Job in a Recession**

By: Learn2succeed.com
Incorporated

With huge increases in job losses, many people are finding it impossible to find work. Students who are graduating from school, college or university are facing challenges like never before. This book will guide all of them through the process of working for themselves; where to get ideas and how to go about it. It is full of practical tips.

140 pages, softcover; ISBN 978-1-55270-382-3 CIP
Canada: $24.95 US: $24.95 UK: £15.79

**For details visit our Canadian Web site: *www.ProductivePublications.ca*
American Web site: *www.ProductivePublications.com*
Order securely online or mail the order form at the end of this catalogue
Phone our Order Desk toll-free at: 1-(877) 879-2669**

eBay for Beginners in Canada

How to Buy and Sell at Auctions

By: Learn2succeed.com Incorporated

This timely book will help every Canadian who wants to buy and sell on eBay. It covers issues specific to Canada (unlike most other books which are written for Americans). Selling on eBay is probably one of the easiest ways for you to earn extra income, yet many people do not know how to go about it. This book will provide you with the basic knowledge to get started with a very small investment.

146 pages, softcover, ISBN 978-1-55270-326-7 CIP
Canada: $24.95 US: $24.95 UK: £15.79

Steps to Starting a Successful eBay Business in Canada

Your Path to Financial Independence

By: Learn2succeed.com Incorporated

This book will help every Canadian who wants to start a business using eBay. It outlines 12 basic steps for success and covers issues specific to Canada (unlike most other books which are written for Americans). Welcome to the World's Largest Auction! Learn how eBay started; how big it has grown and the basics of selling by auction on eBay.

142 pages, softcover, ISBN 978-1-55270-327-4 CIP
Canada: $24.95 US: $24.95 UK: £15.79

eBay Your Own Home-based Business

Practical Steps to Achieve Financial Independence

By: Learn2succeed.com Incorporated

Written in non-technical language, this book will help you make effective use of eBay to run your own home-based business and make money. You can operate either as a part-time or full-time business. It is written from a Canadian perspective and shows you how to get started with a very small investment. This book starts with an eBay primer and tells you what you can sell and how auctions work. It also shows you the role of eBay in the product cycle

182 pages, softcover, ISBN 978-1-55270-329-8 CIP
Canada: $29.95 US: $29.95 UK: £18.99

Expand Your Canadian Business Using eBay

Everything Managers Need to Know to Start Successfully

By: Learn2succeed.com Incorporated

Written in non-technical language, this book will help every Canadian small business person make effective use of eBay to increase their sales to domestic and foreign markets. It covers issues specific to Canadians (unlike most other books which are written for Americans). Selling on eBay is probably one of the easiest ways to test new products and sell-off excess inventory or end-of-line goods, yet many Canadian businesspeople do not know how to go about it. This book will provide them with the basic knowledge to get started with a very small investment.

226 pages, softcover, ISBN 978-1-55270-328-1 CIP
Canada: $34.95 US: $34.95 UK: £21.99

For details visit our Canadian Web site: *www.ProductivePublications.ca*
American Web site: *www.ProductivePublications.com*
Order securely online or mail the order form at the end of this catalogue
Phone our Order Desk toll-free at: 1-(877) 879-2669

The Small Business Guide to Increasing Your Sales Using eBay

Easy Ways to Expand into Domestic and Foreign Markets

By: Learn2succeed.com Incorporated

Written in non-technical language, this book will demonstrate eBay's role in the product cycle so that every business can make effective use of eBay to increase their sales in domestic and foreign markets. How to list products for auction and get paid. How to open an eBay Store. How to get positive feedback and integrate eBay into existing operations.

138 pages, softcover, ISBN 978-1-55270-251-2 CIP
Canada: $24.95 US: $24.95 UK: £15.79

Start Your Own Successful Home-Based Business Using eBay

Everything You Need to Know to Get Started

By: Learn2succeed.com Incorporated

How to start your own full-time or part-time home-based business using eBay. How to register your business, find products, conduct research, list your items for auctions, open an eBay Store and get paid. How to select the right computer hardware and software to help you. The importance of getting positive feedback.

226 pages, softcover, ISBN 978-1-55270-250-5 CIP
Canada: $29.95 US: $29.95 UK: £18.99

Inexpensive E-Commerce Solutions for Small & Home-Based Businesses:

You Don't Have to Spend a Fortune to Start Selling Online

By: Learn2succeed.com Incorporated

Inexpensive E-Commerce Solutions for Small & Home-Based Businesses

This book is a great place to start if you want to learn about inexpensive e-commerce solutions for your small or home-based business. Find out how to do it inexpensively for about $100 per month. You don't have to spend a fortune to start selling online!

130 pages, softcover;; ISBN 978-1-55270-118--8 CIP
Canada: $24.95 US: $24.95 UK: £15.79

Fundamentals of Effective Online Selling

Use the Power of the Internet to Increase Your Sales

By: Learn2succeed.com Incorporated

How to advertise and sell your products or services on the Web. The basics of online selling and some of the challenges facing online merchants. How to use the Web for your market research and how to prepare your Web marketing plan. Take a tour of inexpensive software to establish your own e-commerce Web site. This book will provide you with all the information you need to start increasing your online sales.

206 pages, softcover; ISBN: 978-1-55270-210-9 CIP
Canada: $29.95 US: $29.95 UK: £18.99

For details visit our Canadian Web site: *www.ProductivePublications.ca*
American Web site: *www.ProductivePublications.com*
Order securely online or mail the order form at the end of this catalogue
Phone our Order Desk toll-free at: 1-(877) 879-2669

Inexpensive Ways to Start Your Own Successful Home-Based E-Commerce Business

How to Set Up Your Business, Select Products & Start Selling Online for Well Under $2,000

By: Learn2succeed.com Inc.

How to start your own online business. Where to get ideas and how to check them out. How to plan your business. How much money will you need? How to get financing. How to advertise and sell your products or services on the Web. The basics of online selling and some of the challenges facing online merchants. How to use the Web for your market research and how to prepare your Web marketing plan.

328 pages, softcover; ISBN 978-1-55270-203-1   CIP
Canada: $39.95; USA: $39.95; UK: £25.19

Steps to Starting a Successful Business in the Digital Age

How to Use the Latest Technology to Turn Your Ideas into Money

By: Learn2succeed.com Incorporated

This book will help everyone who wants to start a business in the digital age. It outlines 10 basic steps for success. How to find ideas for a business, conduct market research, create your own Web site and select your e-commerce software. How to set up your business.

144 pages, softcover, ISBN 978-1-55270-301-4   CIP
Canada: $24.95 US: $24.95 UK: £15.79

MAKE IT ON YOUR OWN!

How to Succeed in Your Own Business

By: Barrie Jackson

What it takes to run a business and make it succeed. Contains practical, hands-on information, for immediate use. Learn from the author's personal experience and mistakes. Lots of anecdotes from the author's business adventures which make for interesting reading with a "practical punch".

Before his untimely death, Barrie Jackson, forged Cooper Boating Centre into Canada's largest yacht charter company.

212 pages, softcover; ISBN 978-1-896210-37-7   CIP
Canada: $29.95 US: $29.95 UK: £18.99

Savvy Women Entrepreneurs

Twenty-Eight Different Women Share the Secrets To Their Business Success

By: Kristina Liehr

You don't have to go to business school to start a business! Learn how 28 remarkable women entrepreneurs started their own business; many in their garage or kitchen. Read about the steps that they took; the obstacles they overcame and the joy, happiness and success that they achieved. The chances they took and how they learned from their mistakes. Get the confidence and inspiration to start YOUR own business or EARN EXTRA INCOME.

140 pages, softcover; ISBN 978-1-55270-000-6   CIP
Canada: $24.95 US: $24.95 UK: £15.79

For details visit our Canadian Web site: *www.ProductivePublications.ca*
American Web site: *www.ProductivePublications.com*
Order securely online or mail the order form at the end of this catalogue
Phone our Order Desk toll-free at: 1-(877) 879-2669

Steps to Starting and Running a Successful Business in CANADA

By: Don Lunny

Managing your own business can be a rewarding experience but survival can be tough in today's economy. This book shows you the essential steps to ensure that your business is profitable.

Author, **Don Lunny**, is an experienced business owner and consultant with many years of experience.

190 pages, softcover ISBN 978-0-920847-85-5 CIP
Canada: $34.95

Checklist for Going into Business

By: Don Lunny

Points to create your own checklist to create a profitable business. Starting it is reality. But, there is often a gap between your dream and reality - that can only be filled with careful planning. You need a plan to avoid pitfalls, to achieve your goals and make profits. This guide helps you prepare a comprehensive business plan and determine if your idea is feasible. **Don Lunny** is an experienced business owner and consultant with many years of experience.

53 pages, softcover; ISBN 978-0-920847-86-2 CIP
Canada: $19.95 US: $19.95 UK: £12.59

A Street Wise Manager's Guide to Success in the Restaurant Business

By: Matthew Lallo

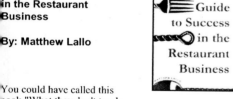

You could have called this book "What they don't teach you at The Culinary Institute". As you know, operating a restaurant is a difficult; even a dangerous business. Competition is fierce and costs keep rising. You are subject to a patchwork of government regulations. You will find it a challenge to succeed in this industry, however, this book can help you to greatly improve your chances. It provides you with a pragmatic view of an industry that is unique and it offers you with unorthodox (but proven) advice on the subtle art of survival.

241 pages, softcover; ISBN 978-1-55270-144-7 CIP
Canada: $29.95 US: $29.95 UK: £16.98

You Can Be Rich!

Eight Easy-to-Remember Principles You Can Use to Create Wealth and Achieve Financial Independence

By: Stuart Mathews

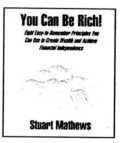

This book is not a get rich quick scheme. It offers an introduction to practical systems of making money. It contains over 20 years of close study into the subject of attaining and holding on to financial wealth. Anyone can become rich or financially independent, but not everyone will. Becoming wealthy will depend on your willingness to identify, learn, and follow financial guidelines and principles. Stuart Mathews shows you how to do this.

174 pages, softcover; ISBN: 978-1-55270-255-0 CIP
Canada: $26.95 US: $29.95 UK: £16.99

For details visit our Canadian Web site: *www.ProductivePublications.ca*
American Web site: *www.ProductivePublications.com*
Order securely online or mail the order form at the end of this catalogue
Phone our Order Desk toll-free at: 1-(877) 879-2669

Page 13

Entrepreneurship and
Starting a Business

Confederation College
Entrepreneurship Series

The Entrepreneur
and the Business Idea

Confederation College
Entrepreneurship Series

Entrepreneurship and Starting a Business provides a comprehensive introduction to entrepreneurs and what they do, and is a must-read for anyone who has aspirations to start and run their own business. The book examines entrepreneurs, their values and behaviour, and factors that contribute to their success and failure. It also takes an in-depth look at how they spot business opportunities or come up with business ideas.

110 pages, softcover; ISBN 978-1-55270-090-7 CIP
Canada: $24.95 US: $24.95 UK: £15.79

If you ever wondered what entrepreneurs are like; where they look for business ideas and opportunities, and what kinds of thinking and tools some of them use in their approach to a possible business start-up, then this introductory book should prove very helpful to you. It includes both a self-assessment and a business opportunity assessment tool, and advocates a "damage control approach" to getting into business.

50 pages, softcover; ISBN 978-1-55270-089-1 CIP
Canada: $14.95 US: $14.95 UK: £9.49

Business Planning
and Finances

Confederation College
Entrepreneurship Series

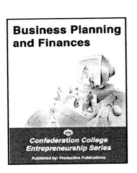

Small Business Finance

Confederation College
Entrepreneurship Series

Business Planning and Finances takes a pragmatic and hands-on approach to business planning and financial management, and is written in straightforward language free of technical jargon. It includes a thorough review of the role of planning, the benefits to be realized from planning, and the use of a plan as a management aid.

174 pages, softcover; ISBN 978-1-55270-091-4 CIP
Canada: $34.95 US: $34.95 UK: £21.99

Small Business Finance was designed with the start-up business owner/manager in mind and provides a detailed overview of the organization and operation of a business from a financial perspective. Developed as a combination textbook and workbook, it takes the reader step-by-step through each element of a company's finances from pre-startup costs all the way to record keeping and financial monitoring for an established business.

136 pages, softcover; ISBN 978-1-55270-092-1 CIP
Canada: $29.95 US: $29.95 UK: £18.89

For details visit our Canadian Web site: *www.ProductivePublications.ca*
American Web site: *www.ProductivePublications.com*
Order securely online or mail the order form at the end of this catalogue
Phone our Order Desk toll-free at: 1-(877) 879-2669

Youth Entrepreneurship

Confederation College Entrepreneurship Series

Some of North America's most successful businesses have been started by people between the ages of 15 and 25. If you are a young person with a business idea or a desire to start your own business then this informative and practical book should be a "must-read" for you. Learn from the experiences of others and improve your prospects for success.

108 pages, softcover; ISBN 978-1-55270-094-5   CIP
Canada: $24.95 US: $24.95 UK: £15.79

Business Relationships – Development and Maintenance

Confederation College Entrepreneurship Series

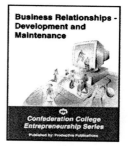

The success of any business hinges on the effective management of three critical categories of business relationships. These are a firm's relationships with its customers, with its employees, and with the individuals and organizations that supply it with essential goods and services. This book outlines the nature and role of each type of relationship, and identifies a variety of best practices and operating tools to be employed in the successful development and maintenance of these relationships.

78 pages; softcover; ISBN 978-1-55270-093-8   CIP
Canada: $19.95 US: $19.95 UK: £12.59

Becoming Successful!

Taking Your Home-Based Business to a New Level

By: Don Varner

Strategies for getting great results in your home-based business! How to turn any type of business into a SUCCESSFUL business!

- Self-Improvement
- Handling Rejections
- Management Skills
- 16 Ways to Prospect
- Designing Great Ads
- Self-Motivation
- Hiring Tips
- Motivating Employees
- Closing Sales
- No-Cost Ways to Advertise

338 pages, softcover; ISBN 978-1-896210-87-2   CIP
Canada: $39.95 US: $39.95 UK: £25.19

Start Your Own Business: Be Your Own Boss!

Your Road Map to Independence

By: Iain Williamson

Learn from someone who has done it! What it takes! Where to get ideas and how to check them out. How to research the market. Calculate how much money you will really need and where to get it. Growing pains and managing employees... plus lots more. Iain Williamson has run his own businesses for over 35 years and is a consultant. He'll help you with a Road Map to Independence!

208 pages, softcover; ISBN 978-1-896210-96-4   CIP
Canada: $29.95 US: $29.95 UK: £18.99

For details visit our Canadian Web site: www.ProductivePublications.ca
American Web site: www.ProductivePublications.com
Order securely online or mail the order form at the end of this catalogue
Phone our Order Desk toll-free at: 1-(877) 879-2669

Can You Make Money with Your Idea or Invention?

By: Don Lunny

- Can you exploit it?
- How to produce it.
- Can you make money?
- Where to get help.
- Industrial Design.
- Copyright.
- Points of caution.
- Patent applications.
- Sample licensing agreement.
- Is the idea original?
- How to distribute it.
- Can you protect it?
- A word about patents.
- Trademarks.
- First steps.
- Possible problems.
- What are your chances?

99 pages, softcover; ISBN 978-0-920847-65-7 CIP
Canada: $24.95 US: $24.95 UK: £15.79

The Canadian Business Guide to Patents for Inventions and New Products

By: George Rolston

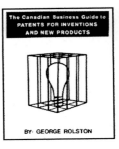

This is your complete reference to patenting around the world. The key elements in the patent process. When to search for earlier patents. When you should file patent applications. The importance of your patent filing date. Understand the critical wording of patent claims. Getting the best out of your patent agent. What the patent office will do for you. What to do if your patent application is rejected. How to go about patenting in foreign countries and how to negotiate a licence agreement. **George Rolston**, is a barrister and solicitor who has specialized in patents for over 30 years.

202 pages, softcover; ISBN 978-0-920847-13-8 CIP
Canada: $48.00

Protect Your Intellectual Property

An International Guide to Patents, Copyrights and Trademarks

By: Hoyt L. Barber & Robert M. Logan

An abundance of information on step-by-step procedures to obtain exclusive protection for unique ideas, inventions, names, identifying marks, or artistic, literary, musical, photographic or cinematographic works. Hoyt Barber is an executive with extensive experience in intellectual property protection. Robert Logan is a practicing U.S. attorney.

305 pages, softcover; ISBN 978-1-896210-95-7 CIP
Canada: $59.95 US: $59.95 UK: £37.79

Evaluating Franchise Opportunities

By: Don Lunny

Although the success rate for franchisee-owned businesses is better than for many other start-up businesses, success is not guaranteed. Don't be "pressured" into a franchise that is not right for you. Investigate your options. How to evaluate the business, the franchisor, the franchise package, and yourself. Author and business consultant, **Don Lunny**, shows you how to avoid the pitfalls before you make a franchise investment.

75 pages, softcover; ISBN 978-0-920847-64-0 CIP
Canada: $19.95 US: $19.95 UK: £12.59

For details visit our Canadian Web site: *www.ProductivePublications.ca*
American Web site: *www.ProductivePublications.com*
Order securely online or mail the order form at the end of this catalogue
Phone our Order Desk toll-free at: 1-(877) 879-2669

Basic Beancounting

Learn to Ape
a Professional
Bookkeeper

By: T. James Cook, CA

This book is intended to help non-accountants understand basic bookkeeping principles and procedures so that they can maintain a simple set of accounting records for a small business. The benefits are up-to-date financial records plus a cost savings by doing a portion of the work that would otherwise be performed by a professional accountant.

121 pages, softcover; ISBN 978-1-55270-204-8 CIP
Canada: $26.95 US: $26.95 UK: £16.99

Gorilla Accounting

How to Survive in a
Jungle of Numbers

By: T. James Cook, CA

Designed to teach the small business owner or manager to read and understand financial statements, and use financial management tools including trend, ratio, and break-even analysis to get maximum information from financial records. Financial and cash flow forecasting are explained and how to use the financial statements effectively. Easy to read, easy to understand, and easy to put into practice.

113 pages, softcover; ISBN 978-1-55270-205-5 CIP
Canada: $26.95

Salary Administration

By:
Entrepreneurial Business
Consultants of Canada

Salary Administration Program provides the means for management to:

- Properly analyse and evaluate positions.
- Provide equitable and competitive remuneration.
- Appraise individual performance in a position.

64 pages; softcover; ISBN 978-1-55270-085-3 CIP
Canada: $39.95 US: $39.95 UK: £25.19

Shoplifting, Security,
Curtailing Crime -
Inside & Out

By: Don Lunny

If you are a shopkeeper or business owner, this practical, hands-on book will alert you to the alarming theft rates you may be exposed to. From petty theft, bad cheques to armed robbery, you get advice on dealing with the situation and how to train staff. Discusses internal theft by employees - how you can recognize it and how to reduce it. If it alerts you to just one problem, it could pay for itself many, many times over.

115 pages; softcover; ISBN 978-0-920847-66-4 CIP
Canada: $29.95 US: $29.95 UK: £18.99

For details visit our Canadian Web site: *www.ProductivePublications.ca*
American Web site: *www.ProductivePublications.com*
Order securely online or mail the order form at the end of this catalogue
Phone our Order Desk toll-free at: 1-(877) 879-2669

Page 17

Marketing for Beginners

How to Get Your Products into the Hands of Consumers

By: Iain Williamson

Covers the basics of marketing for new entrepreneurs. How to make people aware of your products. How to get them to buy. How to get products into the hands of consumers. Traditional channels of distribution versus direct marketing. One-on-one marketing versus mass marketing. Take a look at the Internet as a marketing tool. Ways to promote and advertise your products. After-sales service and the lifetime value of your customers. Sources of marketing information. The author has been marketing products for 20 years.

215 pages, softcover; ISBN 978-1-896210-97-1 CIP
Canada: $29.95 US: $29.95 UK: £18.99

Marketing Beyond 2000

Why You Will Have to Use the Internet to Market Your Goods or Services in the 21st Century

By: Iain Williamson

The Internet will become an awesome marketing tool in the 21st. Century. Learn how its current limitations are being overcome. Take a look at the future of radio, TV and newspapers.

Glimpse at the marketplace of the future. The author says it's up to you to take advantage of this tremendous marketing tool. Find out how!

194 pages, softcover; ISBN 978-1-896210-66-7 CIP
Canada: $27.95 US: $27.95 UK: £17.69

Successful Direct Mail Marketing in Canada

A Step-by-Step Guide to Selling Your Products or Services Through the Mail

By: Iain Williamson

Techniques to make money in the highly competitive direct mail market. Direct mail as an inexpensive way to reach customers. Ways to keep your costs to a minimum. How to save on postage by using bulk rates. How to get the most out of your computer. The author has over 15 years experience selling by direct mail.

114 pages, softcover; ISBN 978-1-896210-39-1 CIP
Canada: $19.95

Jump Start Your New Employees

Get the Most Out of New Hires From Their First Day on the Job!

By: Julie Olley

An organizational tool for various employee transitions with suggested steps to boost initial productivity of new employees from their first day on the job; to minimize the impact on your customers and identify training needs. Also, to professionally handle departing employees while maintaining security and company property. How employee transitions can be used to create a positive impact on your customers.

Olley: 64 pages, softcover; ISBN 1-55270-084-4 CIP
Canada: $12.95 USA: $9.95 UK: £8.19

For details visit our Canadian Web site: *www.ProductivePublications.ca*
American Web site: *www.ProductivePublications.com*
Order securely online or mail the order form at the end of this catalogue
Phone our Order Desk toll-free at: 1-(877) 879-2669

The Six Sigma Toolbox

54 Improvement Tools and When to Use Them

By: Jerry W. Wishes

In this book Jerry Wishes provides fifty-four improvement tools. They are focused around two concepts. First, Variation is Evil. Every process has variation but the secret is to restrict it to natural causes and then use improvement tools to "manage" the variation. Second, use of the tools is not optional. Once you embrace them, you do so forever.

306 pages, softcover; ISBN 978-1-55270-258-1   CIP
Canada: $48.95 US: $48.95 UK: £30.99

Quality in the 21ˢᵗ Century

What You Have to Change to Stay in Business

By: Jerry W. Wishes

Jerry Wishes says: "If you don't 'get it' soon and start doing things differently, you'll be in a down-cycle and never understand why." His hope is that this book will give you some insight and a direction you can use to conquer the challenges ahead.

202 pages, softcover; ISBN 978-1-55270-259-8   CIP
Canada: $39.95 US: $39.95 UK: £25.19

Seven Sigma

The Pursuit of Perfection

By: Jerry W. Wishes

This book makes the case, through the use of a fictional business story, for the rejection of mediocrity in the corporate world. The acceptance of 'things just go wrong' is replaced with the need to raise the bar on expectations. The story takes place at a high-technology start-up.

240 pages, softcover; ISBN: 978-1-55270-260-8   CIP
Canada: $42.95 US: $42.95 UK: £26.99

Modern Materials Management Techniques:

A Complete Guide to Help You Plan, Direct and Control the Purchase, Production, Storage and Distribution of Goods in Today's Competitive Business Environment –Essentials of Supply Chain Management

By: Paula Mackie   **SECOND EDITION**

Covers the entire process of a company's operations relating to the acquisition of goods and services. Written for the public and private sectors as well as college and university educators.

398 pages, softcover; ISBN: 978-1-55270-257-4   CIP
Canada: $74.95 US: $74.95 UK: £47.29

Innovate or Perish!

**Seven-Step Innovation
Process to Meet
the Challenges
of Globalization**

By: Richard Sussman Sc.D.

A complete manual for manufacturing companies to produce new products and processes that can enhance their competitive position. The process starts with the creation of a strategic innovation plan and then provides a system to evaluate the current products and manufacturing capabilities of a company. Methods to select and execute the new developments in the most effective manner. Outsourcing and executive management are reviewed. Dr. Richard Sussman was one of the top technical leaders in the steel industry.

242 pages, softcover, ISBN 978-1-55270-253-6 CIP
Canada: $49.95 US: $49.95 UK: £21.49

Effective Management:

**Interpersonal Skills that
Will Help You Earn
the Respect and
Commitment of Employees**

By: Dave Day Ph.D.

Ten key interpersonal skills for the manager... from choosing a leadership style to the day of completing annual performance evaluations. Contains practical suggestions to increase the productivity and commitment of all employees. Essential reading for all new managers and a resource for existing managers. Dave Day has over 35 years experience as a manager, consultant and Professor of Management at Columbia College.

180 pages, softcover; ISBN 978-1-896210-99-5 CIP
Canada: $27.95 US: $27.95 UK: £17.69

**Critical Analysis
in Decision-Making:**

**Conventional and
"Outside the Box"
Approaches to
Developing Solutions
to Today's Business
Challenges**

By: James Briggs

This book examines why some people make good business decisions more effectively, more often, than others. Great leaders in the public service, business, and the non-profit sectors, remind us that an effective decision-making process is the key to solving problems for any organization. Effective organizations search for leaders who have good problem solving skills.

234 pages, softcover; ISBN 978-1-55270-116-4 CIP
Canada: $48.95 US: $48.95 UK: £30.99

**Project Management:
Welcome Opportunity
or Awesome Burden?**

By: Robert G. Edwards

This concise, how-to, self-help guide will help both aspiring and practicing project managers. Its content was developed during the author's forty-four years in professional engineering and project management. The principles and practices that he describes are based on his personal experience and can easily be applied to most simple or complex projects.

170 pages, softcover; ISBN 978-1-55270-086-0 CIP
Canada: $26.95 US: $26.95 UK: £16.99

**For details visit our Canadian Web site: *www.ProductivePublications.ca*
American Web site: *www.ProductivePublications.com*
Order securely online or mail the order form at the end of this catalogue
Phone our Order Desk toll-free at: 1-(877) 879-2669**

Cooperative Time Management

Get More Done and Have More Fun!

By: Chance Massaro Katheryn Allen-Katz

Contains the wisdom of the last fifty years of research and writing about time management together with eighteen years working in organizations helping people get the most satisfying results. It is intended for people who have goals and want to achieve them. It is interactive and easy to use. The authors are time management experts. Follow the steps which they outline in this 224 page workbook and YOUR RESULTS WILL BE REMARKABLE!

224 pages, softcover; ISBN 978-1-896210-86-5 CIP
Canada: $34.95 US: $34.95 UK: £21.99

LEAN PRODUCTION

How to Use the Highly Effective Japanese Concept of Kaizen to Improve Your Efficiency

By: Jim Thompson

Learn specific techniques and behaviours to improve your effectiveness. Find out about a system that has been used very effectively at the organizational level for over forty years. Author, **Jim Thompson** has held senior management positions with General Motors and the Walker Manufacturing Company.

146 pages, softcover; ISBN 978-1-896210-42-1 CIP
Canada: $24.95 US: $24.95 UK: £15.79

THE LEAN OFFICE

How to Use Just-in-Time Techniques to Streamline Your Office

By: Jim Thompson

This book is for everyone who works in an office. Find out how to foster and nurture employee involvement and put excitement back into continuous improvement. Get the tools needed to improve office productivity. Most importantly, reduce employee stress and frustration, while improving productivity. Find out how this happens with employees, not to employees! Jim Thompson is a lean production consultant who studied these systems first-hand while with GM and Toyota in California.

138 pages, softcover; ISBN 978-1-896210-41-4 CIP
Canada: $24.95 US: $24.95 UK: £15.79

LEAN PRODUCTION FOR THE OFFICE

Common Sense Ideas To Help Your Office Continuously Improve

By: Jim Thompson

More ideas for everyone who works in an office:

- Be idea-driven
- Reduce frustration
- Add value
- Let others benchmark you

How to use employees' creativity and ingenuity. Employees' feelings **do** count! Author, **Jim Thompson**, is the guru of applying lean production to the office environment.

136 pages, softcover; ISBN 978-1-55270-025-9 CIP
Canada: $24.95 US: $24.95 UK: £15.79

For details visit our Canadian Web site: *www.ProductivePublications.ca*
American Web site: *www.ProductivePublications.com*
Order securely online or mail the order form at the end of this catalogue
Phone our Order Desk toll-free at: 1-(877) 879-2669

Speak Up!

Helpful Tips for Business People who Need to Speak in Public

By: T. James Cook, CA

Helps business people improve their speaking skills and become good oral communicators. Includes an assessment of present skills together with practice sessions. Better speaking skills will lead you to more responsibility, authority, and material benefits. Confidence in your speaking skills will result in reduced stress levels when you know that you are going to have to speak, or when you are in a potential speaking situation. Ideas that are well articulated are always given more weight and make you more successful.

110 pages, softcover; ISBN 978-1-55270-256-7 CIP
Canada: $24.95 US: $24.95 UK: £15.79

Quick Fixes for Business Writing

An Eight-Step Editing Process to Find and Correct Common Readability Problems

By: Jim Taylor

Breaks down the editorial process into a series of tasks which are designed to improve the readability of the final product. It will be invaluable to you; regardless of whether you are a novice or a proficient editor. Author, Jim Taylor, has taught Eight-Step Editing for 18 years and clients for his workshops include the Editor's Association of Canada and the Ontario Cabinet Office.

156 pages, softcover; ISBN 978-1-55270-252-9 CIP
Canada: $24.95 US: $ 24. 95 UK: £15.79

Training Your Board of Directors

A Manual for the CEOs, Board Members, Administrators and Executives of Corporations, Associations, Non-Profit and Religious Organizations

By: ArLyne Diamond, Ph.D.

For more than ten years now the author has been training boards of directors of organizations of all kinds, from religious organizations to fast-growing high tech companies. This manual is different from most board training books. It is a combination of short informative pieces and a series of interactive exercises designed to enable the participants to actively reach the desired conclusions rather than being lectured to, or corrected by "the expert."

350 pages, softcover; ISBN 978-1-55270-207-9 CIP
Canada: $39.95 US: $39.95 UK: £25.19

Leadership with Panache

52 Ways to Set Yourself Apart as a Dynamic Manager

By: Jeff Jernigan

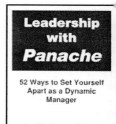

This book cuts to the underbelly of leadership in the modern organization. Divided into 52 "Ways" so that you can select one topic each week of the year for group discussion with your management and supervisory associates. Poses hard hitting questions for consideration. Author, **Jeff Jernigan**, has over 25-years experience as an organizational development specialist providing companies support in creating, continuing and capitalizing on change. He is the recipient of numerous industry awards.

180 pages, softcover; ISBN 978-1-55270-081-5 CIP
Canada: $29.95 US: $29.95 UK: £18.99

For details visit our Canadian Web site: www.ProductivePublications.ca
American Web site: www.ProductivePublications.com
Order securely online or mail the order form at the end of this catalogue
Phone our Order Desk toll-free at: 1-(877) 879-2669

ow to Deliver Excellent ustomer Service

Step-by-Step Guide or Every Business

y: Julie Olley

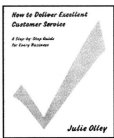

pre-designed workbook pproach for businesses that ish to develop, implement, analyse and follow-up customer ervice projects. Step-by-step "HOW TO:" ideas and sample ormats are included. The suggestions can be implemented ver time. Author, **Julie Olley**, was formerly National **M**anager of Quality Assurance with a major international avel organization. She has designed several curricula for The anadian School of Management and International Business.

60 pages, softcover; ISBN 978-1-55270-045-7 CIP anada: $26.95 US: $26.95 UK: £16.99

Anybody Can Sell!

Sales Strategies to Increase Your Business Profits

By: Don Varner

Written for those who have started a business and have limited selling experience.

- Covers creative marketing and sales presentations.
- Hints on self-motivation and how to handle rejection.
- Discusses different kinds of buyers and how to handle them.

102 pages, softcover; ISBN 978-1-55270-004-4 CIP Canada: $18.95 US: $18.95 UK: £11.99

ecrets of Successful dvertising and romotion

ractical Steps to rowing Your Business

y: Don Varner

Covers all the basics of advertising and promoting for business. How to prospect for more customers. How to increase the average size of your sales.

uthor, **Don Varner**, is an expert with many years of xperience in this area.

58 pages; softcover ISBN 978-1-55270-002-0 CIP anada: $24.95 US: $24.95 UK: £15.79

Timeless Strategies to Become a Successful Entrepreneur

By: Lawrence Scott Troemel

This book is all about starting, building, and managing a small business. The approaches covered in this book have been successfully implemented for decades and will continue to be viable well into the future. Every entrepreneur will benefit from the advice in this very readable book. It is also full of interesting anecdotes.

208 pages; softcover; ISBN 978-1-55270-046-4 CIP Canada: $29.95 US: $29.95 UK: £18.99

**For details visit our Canadian Web site: www.ProductivePublications.ca
American Web site: www.ProductivePublications.com
Order securely online or mail the order form at the end of this catalogue
Phone our Order Desk toll-free at: 1-(877) 879-2669**

The Glass Slipper

Smart Steps for Every Businesswoman's Success

By: Shelley Peever and Layla Didmon

The Glass Slipper is a functional business guide specifically geared toward women in small and medium sized businesses. Each chapter is an integral part of an overall guide that will assist women in gathering information to apply to businesses of their own. A case study section appears at the completion of each chapter. This provides a physical example of the tools and resources offered throughout the book.

110 pages, softcover; ISBN 978-1-55270-262-8   CIP
Canada: $24.95 US: $24.95 UK: £15.79

How to Buy or Sell a Business

Questions You Should Ask and How to Get the Best Price

By: Don Lunny

The decision to buy or sell a business requires careful consideration. It may affect the course of the participants future lives. Yet a surprising number of owners rush into transactions without adequate preparation. Find out how to set the price, locate prospects, evaluate offers, close deals and finance purchases. Author, **Donald Lunny,** has many years of business experience and has been involved with the purchase and sale of many businesses.

134 pages, softcover; ISBN 978-1-896210-98-8   CIP
Canada: $24.95 US: $24.95 UK: £15.79

Tips for Entrepreneurs

How to Meet the Challenges of Starting And Managing Your Own Business

By: Henry Kyambalesa

This book is the culmination of a 3-year research study into the challenges faced by entrepreneurs when they become their own boss. Tips for those about to start a business & tips for those already in business. Decide whether self-employment is for you. Practical advice on getting started. The skills you will need. Henry Kyambalesa is a tenured lecturer in Business Administration. He holds B.B.A., M.A., and M.B.A. degrees.

194 pages, softcover ISBN 978-1-896210-85-8   CIP
Canada: $26.95 US: $26.95 UK: £16.99

Work from Your Home Office as an Independent Contractor

A Complete Guide to Getting Started

By: Chantelle Sauer

An independent contractor is someone who works from his or her home or home office e.g., consultants, entrepreneurs, business owners, freelancers and outsourcers. Learn about the advantages and disadvantages as well as the legal obligations. Also get many ideas on how to become an independent contractor. Author, **Chantelle Sauer,** has spent four years as an independent contractor. She knows from first-hand experience how to get work.

166 pages, softcover; ISBN 978-1-55270-077-8   CIP
Canada: $24.95 US: $24.95 UK: £15.79

For details visit our Canadian Web site: *www.ProductivePublications.ca*
American Web site: *www.ProductivePublications.com*
Order securely online or mail the order form at the end of this catalogue
Phone our Order Desk toll-free at: 1-(877) 879-2669

The Basics for Sales Success

An Essential Guide for New Sales Representatives, Entrepreneurs and Business People

By: Bill Sobye

An introductory book which covers the basic points on how to:

- Find customers
- Study your prospects
- Dress for success
- Handle "the butterflies"
- Set goals
- How to include humour
- Success and rejection
- Business versus pleasure

Bill Sobye has 28 years of experience as a Sales Manager.

157 pages; softcover; ISBN 978-1-896210-65-0 CIP
Canada: $24.95 US: $24.95 UK: £15.79

Bulletproof Salesman

A Lively Guide to Enhance Your Sales Techniques

By: Steven Travis Smith & Bruce D. Seymour

Strategies to Help You Bridge the Gap Between Textbook Training and the Real World

A humorous, yet practical guide written using a tag-team approach between the authors. It explains how they've completely screwed-up over the years avoided making the same mistakes again. Learn from their failures as well as their victories. They explain how to reach absolutely anyone, evade the traps constructed to keep salespeople out, and how to instantly detect deception during negotiations.

231 pages, softcover; ISBN 978-1-55270-209-3 CIP
Canada: $29.95 $US: $29.95 £18.99

Software for Small Business 2011 Edition

Windows & Vista Programs to Help you Improve Business Efficiency and Productivity

By: Iain Williamson

Reviews of 240 programs for new and experienced users. Covers operating systems, word processing, desktop publishing, voice dictation, graphics, digital photography, digital video & audio, spreadsheets, accounting, databases, contact management, communications, internet software, security and virus protection.

472 pages, softcover; ISBN978-1-55270-405-9 CIP
ISSN: 1492-384X Canada: $79.95 US: $79.95 UK: £50.49

Learn UNIX in Fifteen Days

By: Dwight Baer and Paul Davidson

This book was written out of the need for a text which presents the material which is actually taught in a typical UNIX course at the college level. It is not intended to replace a comprehensive UNIX manual, but for most students who have not yet spent five years learning all the "eccentricities" of the UNIX Operating System, it will present all they need to know (and more!) in order to use and support a UNIX system.

176 pages, softcover; ISBN: 978-1-55270-087-7 CIP
Canada: $34.95 US: $34.95 UK: £21.99

Management During an Economic Crisis

Best Practices for Small Business Survival in a Recession

By: Robert Papes

Best practices which are vital to every small business to help them survive the current recession because "hope" of better times is not a viable strategy. This book is all meat and potatoes with no filler. Author, Robert Papes, is a consultant with many years of experience in helping businesses in difficulty.

182 pages, softcover; ISBN 1-55270-384-7 CIP
Canada: $29.95 US: $29.95 UK: £18.99

MAKE IT! MARKET IT! BANK IT!

Over 100 Ways to Start Your Own Home-Based Business

By: Barbara J. Albrecht

This book is about starting your own home-based business. It's also about earning extra money when your wages don't stretch far enough. Money for vacations and education often fall through the cracks in your financial plans and you may find that you need a second income. Newspaper columnist, Barb Albrecht, has assembled these 100 great ideas to help you put cash into your "money jar". If you're looking to run your own part-time business or start a new career as owner of your own enterprise....you must read this book.

144 pages, softcover; ISBN 978-1-55270-145-4 CIP
Canada: $24.95 US: $24.95 UK: £15.79

Your Homebased Business Plan

-Also-

Working With Your Banker

By: Donald Lunny

SECTION I - The Business Plan
for Homebased Business: a step-by-step guide to writing it.

SECTION II - Working with your Banker: the fundamentals of borrowing and how they affect you.

Donald Lunny: an entrepreneur and consultant with many years experience in organizing and restructuring companies.

52 pages, softcover; ISBN 978-0-920847-35-0 CIP
Canada: $14.95 US: $14.95 £9.49

THE NET EFFECT

Will the Internet be a Panacea or Curse for Business and Society in the Next Ten Years?

By: Iain Williamson

Are you ready for the greatest change to business & society since the Industrial Revolution? Examine the world ten years from now when entire sectors of the economy may be eliminated and others will be born. Find out who will be the winners and losers and how it will affect you. Prepare for the dramatic changes that are coming!

244 pages, softcover, ISBN 1-896210-38-4; CIP
Canada: $29.95 USA: $21.95 UK: £18.99

For details visit our Canadian Web site: *www.ProductivePublications.ca*
American Web site: *www.ProductivePublications.com*
Order securely online or mail the order form at the end of this catalogue
Phone our Order Desk toll-free at: 1-(877) 879-2669

eath by Food

hy More People in North
merica Die By Food
oisoning than Were
urdered in 9/11

y: Iain Williamson

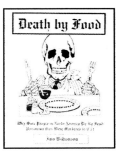

you've ever had food poisoning, you're certainly not alone.
5 million Americans and 12 million Canadians suffer from a
odborne illness **every year**. Food poisoning is now one of
e leading causes of illness in both Canada and the United
ates. Deaths due to foodborne pathogens total about 5,000
nnually for the US. This no-nonsense book claims that the
od you eat may be neither safe nor healthy and suggests
hat you can do about it.

56 pages, softcover; ISBN 978-1-55270-383-0   CIP
anada: $24.95 US: $24.95 UK: £15.79

**Yoga for Mind, Body
and Spirit**

**Details of Practices That
Will Help Your Health,
Psychological
and Spiritual Well-Being**

By: Dr. John R.M. Goyeche

Detailed descriptions of certain yoga practices for physical,
mental and spiritual development; for different-aged people;
for different situations and for people with certain health
concerns. Dr. Goyeche has studied and taught yoga on three
continents and in many settings for over 30 years.

188 pages, softcover; ISBN 978-1-55270-056-3   CIP
Canada: $24.95 US: $24.95 UK: £15.79

inning Over Depression

io-Energetic Therapy
o Overcome Sadness,
ear and Anger

y: Dr. John R.M. Goyeche

straightforward book that discusses the causes of depression.
ffers practical answers to overcome it. Written for the general
ublic and also practitioners of psychiatry, medicine and
ealth care. Dr. John R.M. Goyeche has 25 years of clinical
xperience in hospitals, mental health centres and
habilitation clinics..

30 pages, softcover; ISBN 978-1-55270-051-8   CIP
anada: $24.95 US: $24.98 UK:£15.79

**Benefit From Hypnosis,
Hypnosis by Telephone
and Self-Hypnosis**

**How to Improve Your
Self-Esteem, Creativity
and Performance as well
as Your Spiritual, Physical
and Mental Well-Being**

By: Dr. John R.M. Goyeche

Hypnosis can help you with:
Habits & Addictions
Self-Esteem & Depression
Creative Activity
Memory Retrieval

Fears & Anxieties
General Medical Problems
Spirituality
Performance Enhancement

Dr. Goyeche is a member of the Canadian Society of Clinical
Hypnosis, a Fellow of the International College of
Psychosomatic Medicine, a member of the International
Institute for Bio-Energetic Analysis.

212 pages, softcover; ISBN: 978-1-55270-050-1   CIP
Canada: $21.95 US: $21.95 UK: £13.89

For details visit our Canadian Web site: *www.ProductivePublications.ca*
American Web site: *www.ProductivePublications.com*
Order securely online or mail the order form at the end of this catalogue
Phone our Order Desk toll-free at: 1-(877) 879-2669

Slot Machines: Fun Machines or Tax Machines?

A Technician Reveals the Truth About One-Armed Bandits

By: Ian B. Williams

How slot machines work and how to play them. Covers the pay-out systems. Helps you have a better casino experience. Also examines the social implications of slot machines in our society; both the positive and negative. **Ian B. Williams** is a certified electronics technician and a trained slot technician, who worked for several years in the casino industry.

134 pages, softcover; ISBN 978-1-55270-049-5   CIP
Canada: $24.95 US: $ 24.95 UK: £15.79

Make Money Trading Options

How to Start Immediately

By: Jason Diptee

Want to invest in an expensive stock, the Japanese Yen or the DOW but only have $200- $300 to invest? Option trading allows you to enter these markets to take advantage of investment opportunities that would otherwise require thousands of dollars. This book will teach beginners how to participate in the largely untapped and unknown area of investing that can generate profits in a matter of weeks. Jason Diptee holds an MBA and is an experienced seminar leader on the subject of option trading.

116 pages, softcover; ISBN 978-1-55270-148-5   CIP
Canada: $24.95 US: $24.95 UK: £15.79

Dollars to Donuts

A Personal Wealth Management Model for Canadians

By:Daniel Kesselring

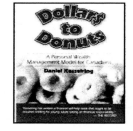

Five Easy Steps that Can Change Your Financial Direction Today

This book provides a unique unbiased perspective from outside the financial services and wealth management industries. It is a product of research, personal observation and a lifetime of trial-and-error experience that led to a system of money management that has served the author extraordinarily well over the years.

157 pages, softcover; ISBN 978-1-55270-208-6   CIP
Canada: $24.95

"You're Hired.... You're Fired!"

A Manager's Guide to Employee Supervision

By: Deborah L. Whitworth

This book is a great read if you are a manager or a supervisor; even if it is only being in charge temporarily for a day. It will provide you with a step-by-step method of acquiring practical human resource management skills.

Author, Deborah L. Whitworth, has been a human resource manager for over 20 years. She believes that management isn't rocket science but a process. You want to do the right thing. Unfortunately, nobody has told you what the right thing is. Deborah acts as a role model and shows you how to manage yourself, so you can be free to manager others.

144 pages, softcover; ISBN 978-1-55270-146-1   CIP
Canada: $24.95 US: $24.95 UK: £15.79

For details visit our Canadian Web site: *www.ProductivePublications.ca*
American Web site: *www.ProductivePublications.com*
Order securely online or mail the order form at the end of this catalogue
Phone our Order Desk toll-free at: 1-(877) 879-2669

**, You Wanna
a Millionaire...**

: James P. Johnson

is book provides you with
step-by-step guide to developing a personalized financial
n that will help you build wealth. The techniques are very
nple to understand and the author has done a great job in
plaining the basic concepts in a straightforward way. He has
cluded many tables that you can immediately use in creating
ur own wealth-building plan.

0 pages, softcover; ISBN: 978-1-55270-088-4 CIP;
nada: $36.95 US: $36.95 UK: £23.29

Short Cut to Easy Street

**How to Get Money in
Your Mailbox Every Day,
Plus Automatic Income
for the Rest of Your Life**

By: Stephen W. Kenyon

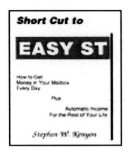

A great book on self-motivation, direct mail, self-publishing,
marketing/advertising/promoting and network marketing.
Study and learn the details of Stephen Kenyon's fascinating
system for attracting wealth and success. He shares with you
the inside trade secrets and techniques which he learned over
a 30-year period.

244 pages, softcover; ISBN 978-1-55270-057-0 CIP
Canada: $37.95 US: $37.95 UK: £23.99

**w to Write a Million Dollar
dventure Novel**

**vel Writing as a
ofitable Profession**

: Dr. Ray Mesluk

structured approach to writing your novel quickly and easily.
aster the techniques of novel writing and turn them into a
ofitable career.

4 pages, softcover; ISBN 978-1-55270-001-3 CIP
nada: $34.95 US: $34.95 UK: £21.99

**The "Please" & "Thank You"
of Fundraising for
Non-Profits:**

**Fifteen Essential
Ingredients for Success**

By: ArLyne Diamond, Ph.D.

This book will show you how to
successfully raise funds for non-
profits; whether you are a member
of a national organization, or a small community association.
The author, Dr. ArLyne Diamond, has many years of
experience with non-profits. She says raising money is an art
form rather than a science. Her book shows you how to do it.

126 pages, softcover; ISBN 978-1-55270-261-1 CIP
Canada $24.95 $US: $24.95 UK:£15.77

For details visit our Canadian Web site: *www.ProductivePublications.ca*
American Web site: *www.ProductivePublications.com*
Order securely online or mail the order form at the end of this catalogue
Phone our Order Desk toll-free at: 1-(877) 879-2669

Page 29

ORDER FORM

Qty.	Title	Price
	ADD Postage: $9.95 first title within Canada or $9.95 to USA	
	ADD $2.25 Postage per title thereafter in Canada or $3.25 to USA	
	SUB-TOTAL	
	ADD 5% HST - Canadian Residents Only (others EXEMPT)	
	TOTAL	

Name_____

Organization_____

Street_____

City/Town_____State/Prov_____ Zip/Postal Code_____

Phone_____Fax_____

☐ Cheque ☐ VISA ☐ MasterCard ☐ American Express

Credit Card Orders: can be faxed to: + (416) 322-7434

Card Number_____

Expiry Date(Month/Year)_____

Cardholder Signature_____

Mail to: **Productive Publications**
PO Box 7200, Stn. A, Toronto, ON M5W 1X8 Canada
Order Desk toll-free: 1-(877) 879-2669 Fax: (416) 322-7434
Order Securely Online at: www.ProductivePublications.ca